The Arts and Crafts Movement

a study of its sources, ideals and influence on design theory

Gillian Naylor

Studio Vista London

To Esca and Tom

© 1971 Gillian Naylor
Designed by Keith Kail
First published in Great Britain 1971 by Studio Vista Publishers
Blue Star House, Highgate Hill, London N19
Set in Monotype Ehrhardt 11/12 pt.
Printed in England
by Richard Clay (The Chaucer Press) Ltd, Bungay, Suffolk
ISBN 0 289 79580 X

Contents

Acknowledgements

Acknowledgements are due to the following for permission to take or reproduce photographs: Victoria and Albert Museum, London; Leicester Museum and Art Gallery, Leicester; Ashmolean Museum, Oxford; The Tate Gallery, London; The Society of Antiquaries; Lady Mander of Wightwick Manor, Wolverhampton; the Governors and staff of Pownall Hall, Cheshire; and the De Morgan Foundation. Mrs. M. Canham of the Kingston Museum and Art Gallery, M. D. E. Clayton-Stamm, Esq., Miss M. Weaver and Mr Richard Sword of the William Morris Gallery were particularly helpful, both in providing material and facilities for photography.

I am indebted to Miss Felicity Ashbee for permission to quote from C. R. Ashbee's unpublished *Memoirs* in the Victoria and Albert Museum Library, and to the London Library who lent books over a long period.

Sincere thanks are also due to Ray Watkinson for his advice and generous loan of books and information; to my colleagues at Brighton and Kingston Polytechnics, and to the staff of Studio Vista for their care, help and patience.

The device reproduced on the title page is C. R. Ashbee's Essex House Press colophon, inspired by the pinks which grew in abundance in the garden of the Guild's Essex House premises in the Mile End Road.

Introduction

The Arts and Crafts movement was inspired by a crisis of conscience. Its motivations were social and moral, and its aesthetic values derived from the conviction that society produces the art and architecture it deserves. It was originally a British movement; Britain, first in the field as the workshop of the world, was the first to discover that factory conditions are far from ideal, and the realization that technical progress does not necessarily coincide with the improvement of man's lot brought with it the long campaign for social, industrial, moral and aesthetic reform that is still unresolved today. The Arts and Crafts movement represents one facet of that campaign, but because the movement marks a stage in man's efforts to come to terms with industrialization, it was not confined to England. Similar attitudes developed in European countries as they industrialized, and in the United States, so that when the theories of Ruskin and Morris and their successors began to reach a wider audience the response they evoked was generally sympathetic, and the products of the British movement were greeted with similar acclaim.

For a brief period at the end of the nineteenth century British design and British design theory enjoyed an unprecedented prestige. To some observers these achievements represented the triumph of individuality: British architects and craftsmen had broken free from the trammels of the past, and had created a new art, a personal aesthetic that would embrace architecture and design as well as the 'fine' arts. The appeal to individuality, fashion and novelty was obvious, but the British promoters of this revival firmly disassociated themselves from the stylistic extravagances of Art Nouveau. Their endeavours were directed, ultimately, towards a social end, the establishment of a society in which all men would enjoy the freedom to be creative. Their concern, therefore, was not focused exclusively on end-products but on the society that shaped them, the men who designed and made them and on the people who bought them. Ashbee perhaps provided the neatest definition of this attitude: 'The Arts and Crafts Movement', he wrote in *Craftsmanship in Competitive Industry* (1908), 'means standards, whether of work or life; the protection of standards, whether in the product or the producer, and it means that these things must be taken together.'

It was this concern to see the problems of design within a social context that was to have the most significant influence on twentieth-century design thinking; Van de Velde, Muthesius, Loos and Gropius, in fact the majority of the 'pioneers' who formulated the principles of the Modern Movement, were all stimulated by British precept and example to work towards the creation of an environment that would both serve and express people's needs. The methods each suggested and the solutions they proposed

7

were in themselves radically different, but their concern was with one common goal—that of 'averting mankind's enslavement to the machine by saving the mass product and the home from mechanical anarchy and by restoring them to purpose, sense and life . . .' (Walter Gropius *The Scope of Total Architecture*).

Fundamental to the British Arts and Crafts philosophy, especially in the first stages of its development, was the conviction that industrialization had brought with it the total destruction of 'purpose, sense and life'. These nineteenth-century idealists had learned to spell out the cost of mechanical 'progress' in terms of human misery and degradation; they saw the destruction of fundamental human values reflected in poverty, overcrowded slums, grim factories, a dying countryside and the apotheosis of the cheap and shoddy. In such conditions, they maintained, the good (and therefore the beautiful), whether in art or life, was strangled at birth. As Morris put it: 'Men living amidst such ugliness cannot conceive of beauty, and, therefore, cannot express it'.[1]

Their rebellion against what they conceived as the indiscriminate exploitation of the many for the profit of the few, led, in Morris's case at least, to a commitment to the idea of revolution; on a less radical plane it led to a rejection, or reinterpretation of the accepted definitions of the design process. For in England the socially aware within the design profession tended to be rebels against orthodox social and academic attitudes, and their non-conformity led to a rugged individualism. Having embraced the Cause, as defined by Ruskin and Morris, each designer learned to forge his own path and establish a personal interpretation of the craft doctrine, so that talents as disparate as those of Crane, Benson, Gimson, Voysey, Mackmurdo, De Morgan, Lethaby and Ashbee were extending the conventions and philosophy of design and ornament, preparing the way, on the one hand, for Art Nouveau, and on the other, through their teaching and incessant personal analyses of the social purposes of design and architecture, for the ideals and dogmatism of the Modern Movement.

These were responsible men, intelligent and sensitive enough to understand that their concern with the values of the past might so conflict with the realities of the present that their work would be rendered useless. Gradually each came to realize—and with each it tended to be a painful process of self-realization—that machinery need not be a destructive force, and that men, as Voysey put it 'must live and work in the present'. But in spite of the fact that many of these designers did work for industry and supported programmes for the improvement of industrial design standards, none of them were in a position to grasp the nature of the forces that were revolutionizing society. Theirs was a personal and subjective approach, and although they came to appreciate intellectually the fact of the machine as the normal tool of our civilization, they were unable, or unwilling, to absorb, as Lewis Mumford has put it, 'the lessons of objectivity, impersonality, neutrality, the lessons of the mechanical realm'.[2] Nor were they as confident as their successors in Gropius's generation that men would be able to direct and control technology, and in this, of course, all the indications are that they will be proved right.

But here lies the paradox of nineteenth-century idealism; once the idea of practical expediency was abandoned, and design reform was considered a Cause and a Crusade, an element of impotence and unreality entered the proceedings. In Britain Ruskin and Morris and their disciples within the Arts and Crafts movement saw the uncontrolled advance of technology as a threat to man's spiritual and physical well-being, but at the same time they had no clearer understanding of the nature of their adversary—industry—than had Henry Cole and his associates. They carried their banner in the name of humanity, but the new society that they envisaged bore so little relationship to contemporary reality, that its delights were a snare and a delusion, and possession of its products confined to an appreciative, affluent and intelligent élite. Both Ruskin and Morris died frustrated men, having spent their lives proselytizing a seemingly indifferent public, and Ashbee, in his unpublished *Memoirs*, defined the nature of his and their dilemma. 'We have made', he wrote, 'of a great social movement, a narrow and tiresome little aristocracy working with great skill for the very rich.'[3]

This ambiguity between their ideals and their achievement was obvious to their successors. Their sympathizers, men like Van de Velde, Muthesius and Gropius, acknowledged the ideal and broke the taboo, attempting to extend the values of the Arts and Crafts movement to machine production. But the idealism was open to misinterpretation and many critics were to ignore the underlying social concern and see the efforts of these nineteenth-century reformers at best as quaint and misguided. As early as 1899, for example, Thorstein Veblen was equating the desire for the hand-made with conspicuous consumption, thus neatly reversing the values that the movement had sought to establish:

'. . . the generic feature of the physiognomy of machine-made goods as compared with the hand-wrought article is their greater perfection in workmanship and greater accuracy in the detail execution of the design. Hence it comes about that the visible imperfections of the hand-wrought goods, being honorific, are accounted marks of superiority in point of beauty, or serviceability, or both. Hence has arisen that exaltation of the defective, of which John Ruskin and William Morris were such eager spokesmen in their time; and on this ground their propaganda of crudity and wasted effort has been taken up and carried forward since their time.'[4]

In the twentieth century their reputation has varied with the response to the idea and ideal of the 'machine' as a redemptive force in society. It reached its lowest ebb, predictably enough, with the Futurists, and the technique-oriented theorists of the '20s and '30s. In 1912, for example, Marinetti urged members of a London audience to

'. . . disencumber yourselves of the lymphatic ideology of your deplorable Ruskin . . . with his hatred of the machine, of steam and electricity, this maniac for antique simplicity resembles a man who in full maturity wants to sleep in his cot again and drink at the breasts of a nurse who has now grown old, in order to regain the carefree state of infancy . . .'[5]

László Moholy-Nagy's *The New Vision* created a new myth by declaring that the 'Ruskin, Morris circle in the 1880s . . . opposed the machine so strongly that, in order to deliver their hand-made products to London, they ran a horse-coach along-side the hated railway';[6] J. J. P. Oud believed that Ruskin and Morris had committed a 'cardinal error' and had 'brought the machine into disrepute by stigmatizing an impure use of it as its essence',[7] and, more recently, Reyner Banham has declared that

'the human chain of pioneers of the Modern Movement that extends back from Gropius to William Morris, and beyond him to Ruskin, Pugin and William Blake, does not extend forward from Gropius. The precious vessel of handicraft aesthetics that has been passed from hand to hand, was dropped and broken, and no one has bothered to pick up the pieces.'[8]

The aim of this book is to examine the nature of the handicraft aesthetic as it developed in England in the nineteenth century, and to outline its impact on design theory in Europe and the United States. The basic hypothesis is that the 'precious vessel' was not shattered but cracked and tarnished, and its purpose misunderstood, and that the attitudes of twentieth-century designers, even those who feel themselves totally alienated from their counterparts in the First Machine Age, are nevertheless still conditioned, for better or worse, by the efforts of these nineteenth-century reformers to create a world fit to live in. The ways and means differ, as does the nature of the compromise between aesthetic, commercial and functional requirements; but the ideal, as defined by Moholy-Nagy[9] remains the same: to 'lay down the basis for an organic system of production whose focal point is man, not profit'.

1　The sources

Contemporary historians of the Arts and Crafts movement were confident of its chronology: T. J. Cobden-Sanderson, whose monograph *The Arts and Crafts Movement* was published in 1905, maintained that the Arts and Crafts Exhibition Society 'initiated the wider movement which, from itself as source, has spread all the world over'; Walter Crane insisted that 'the first practical steps towards actually producing things combining use and beauty and thus enabling people so minded to deck their homes after the older and simpler English manner was [sic] taken by William Morris and his associates'.[1] It is obvious, however, that the forces which shaped the movement were in evidence long before the 1860s, when Morris was establishing his Firm, and the 1880s when the impact of Ruskin's and Morris's teaching crystallized in the Guild ideal and the formation of at least five societies to promote that ideal.

The ideology of the movement has a complex pre-history, based in part on a generation's preoccupation with doctrine and 'style' in architecture and design, and in part on reactions, both positive and negative, to the facts of life in a machine age. During the course of the eighteenth century when British invention was laying the foundations of a new economy, progress was seen by many as the inevitable reward for diligence, energy and skill. For a time the growth of cities and the expansion of industry were welcomed as part of an inevitable progress from which all men would ultimately benefit:

> . . . th' echoing hills repeat
> The stroke of ax and hammer; scaffolds rise,
> And growing edifices; heaps of stone,
> Beneath the chissel, beauteous shapes assume
> Of frize and column. Some, with even line,
> New streets are marking in the neighb'ring fields,
> And sacred domes of worship. Industry,
> which dignifies the artist, lifts the swain,
> And the straw cottage to a palace turns,
> Over the work presides. . . .
> So appear
> Th' increasing walls of busy Manchester,
> Sheffield, and Birmingham, whose redd'ning fields
> Rise and enlarge their suburbs. Lo, in throngs,
> For every realm the careful factors meet,
> Whispering each other[2]

John Dyer's *The Fleece*, a poem in praise of the expanding cotton industry, was published in 1757, and was symptomatic of a certain mid-century optimism—an optimism that was reflected (as the poem indicates) in the self-assurance of neo-classicism. The British design achievement of the late eighteenth century—the *style anglais* as represented by the work of Adam, Hepplewhite, Sheraton and Wedgwood, to name but a few—was admired and imitated in Europe and America, since it combined the virtues of refinement and sophistication with fitness, sobriety and purity of form, and lent itself admirably to semi-craft techniques of production. The growth of industrialization, however, was to choke rather than encourage those very qualities that it had seemed to foster, and by the beginning of the nineteenth century machinery had begun to assume the role of a Frankenstein monster, of man's making, but beyond his control. The romantic poets expressed fears as well as hopes for the Age of Machinery, but the first British writer to apprehend the nature of the forces that were transforming society, and to castigate them with any consistent invective was Carlyle, who defined his position in his essay 'Signs of the Times', published in 1829 in the *Edinburgh Review*:*

'Our old modes of exertion are all discredited, and thrown aside. On every hand the living artisan is driven from his workshop, to make room for a speedier inanimate one. The shuttle drops from the fingers of the weaver, and falls into iron fingers that ply it faster. For all earthly, and for some unearthly purpose, we have machines and mechanic furtherances . . . We remove mountains, and make seas our smooth highway; nothing can resist us. We war with rude Nature; and by our restless engines, come off victorious and loaded with spoils . . . Not the external and physical alone is now managed by machinery, but the internal and spiritual also. Here, too, nothing follows its spontaneous course, nothing is left to be accomplished by old natural methods . . . Men are grown mechanical in head and heart, as well as in hand. They have lost faith in individual endeavour, and in natural force of any kind.'

In a little over a generation, therefore, industry seemed to have outgrown its early promise, and far from being considered a source of rejuvenation and vitality, a tool that would unite and improve mankind, it had come to be seen as a negative force, stultifying both artist and artisan, and destroying England's culture, security and traditions. A concrete rather than intellectual demonstration of such attitudes had already been provided by the descendants of Dyer's 'careful factors'—the Luddites of 1811, and the rural machine wreckers of the 1830s; but although Robert Owen was replanning the New Lanark Mills in 1800 and Cobbett had embarked on his rural rides in 1821, it was not until the 1830s that social and moral considerations began to have any marked influence on aesthetic evaluations.

* It is perhaps worth noting that Carlyle had been engaged in the translation of Goethe's *Wilhelm Meister* since 1824, and in the third book of the *Wanderjahre*, which appeared in its final form in 1829, Wilhelm Meister had declared 'this rapid spread of machinery troubles and frightens me. It is gathering like a storm, slowly, slowly; but it is moving towards us and will come and burst upon us.'

Pugin

The precursor here of attitudes that were to become fundamental to the Arts and Crafts movement was Pugin, and his two most important books *Contrasts*, published in 1836 at his own expense, and *True Principles of Christian Architecture*, published five years later, express ideas that were to become assumptions with the next generation. In fact Pugin's career, as well as his theory, anticipated in several aspects those of many of his successors. His father, Augustus Pugin, had come to England during the French Revolution, and had worked for Nash, drawing the fashionable gothic details that his clients demanded and Nash detested. Augustus Welby Northmore Pugin was born in London in 1812; as a boy he had provided his father with drawings, and when he was only fifteen he was designing silverware for the Royal Goldsmiths, Rundell, Bridge & Rundell, patrons of John Flaxman, and furniture for Morel and Seddon, who were involved in the restoration of Windsor Castle.

Before he was twenty-one, Pugin had worked for two years as a stage designer at Covent Garden—his *pièce de résistance* being the scenery for the opera *Kenilworth*; he had married, had been widowed and had married again; he had set up his own firm for the production of gothic ornament which had failed, whereupon he was imprisoned for debt. In 1835 he was converted to Roman Catholicism; in 1836 he was working with Barry on the Houses of Parliament, and from that time until his death in 1852 he was designing churches and houses, as well as furnishing them. He ran his practice from his own house in Ramsgate, producing stained glass, metalwork, textiles, wallpapers and jewellery (pls 1 and 2) and employing several assistants, including John Hardman Powell (pl 5), nephew of John Hardman, the metal-worker, and a young man who had worked with Overbeck.[3]

Like his successors in the Arts and Crafts movement Pugin was concerned, both in his theory and practice, to combat 'the present decay of taste'; like them he believed that architecture should be 'the expression of existing opinions and circumstances' rather than 'a confused jumble of styles and symbols borrowed from all nations and periods',[4] and he was the first of the Gothicists to relate that style to the spirit that had created it. With Pugin, Gothic became an expression of faith, rather than fashion, a matter of principle rather than style; all his aspirations were directed towards the revival of that faith, and with it the restoration of the Christian spirit which had inspired 'the noble edifices of the Middle Ages'. He believed that before the Reformation, stability and order were reflected in man's surroundings, as well as in his life, and for him 'Catholic England was merry England, at least for the humbler classes; and the architecture was in keeping with the faith and manners of the time—at once strong and hospitable'.[5] Strength and hospitality, he maintained, were remote from the mammon-inspired architecture of his own day: 'The erection of churches', he wrote in *Contrasts*, anticipating Ruskin's lecture on the Bradford exchange by some thirty years, 'like all that was produced by zeal and art in the ancient days, has dwindled into a mere trade . . . They are erected by men who ponder between a mortgage, a railroad or a chapel, as the best investment of their money, and who, when they have resolved on relying on the persuasive eloquence of a cushion thumping, popular

preacher, erect four walls, with apertures for windows, cram the same full of seats . . .'
His convictions might, of course, have been somewhat suspect in an age that was
solidly Protestant, but in elaborating them Pugin formulated principles of propriety
and structural fitness that were to be fundamental to nineteenth-century design theory.
At the beginning of *True Principles* Pugin had written: 'The two great rules for design
are these: 1st, that there should be no features about a building which are not necessary for convenience, construction, or "propriety"; 2nd, that all ornament should
consist of enrichment of the essential construction of the building.' In the course of
his argument he relates these ideas to product design and here his invective against
contemporary malpractices anticipates that of Morris:

'All the ordinary articles of furniture, which require to be simple and convenient, are
made not only very expensive, but very ordinary. We find diminutive flying buttres-
ses about an armchair; everything is crocketed with angular projections, innumerable
mitres, sharp ornaments and turretted extremities. A man who remains any length of
time in a modern Gothic room and escapes without being wounded by some of its
minutiae may consider himself fortunate.'

He castigates the wares spewed out by those 'inexhaustible mines of bad taste, Birmingham and Sheffield'; modern upholstery, he says, 'is made a surprising vehicle for
bad and paltry taste'; silverwork is 'sunk to a mere trade' and 'glaring, showy and
meretricious ornament . . . disgraces every branch of our art and manufactures'.

His objections relate to all non-authentic styles, whether they are gothic or neo-
classic, but neo-classicism was his special anathema, not, as Ruskin was to maintain,
because it was 'mechanical', but because it was the expression of a Pagan rather than
a Christian culture, and therefore unsuitable for nineteenth-century England. The
illustrations to *Contrasts* demonstrate the debasement of what Pugin calls 'architectural propriety' which had accompanied the debasement of faith and humanity. He
depicts nineteenth-century towns, with the sparse façades of the factory, gas-works,
Town Hall, the sewage works and Lunatic Asylum crowding against the ruins of the
Abbey and the Priory; the traditional protectors of the poor, offering hospitality in
their mellowed monasteries, with free gifts of shelter, strong ale, good meat and
cheese, have been replaced by the Acropolis-inspired poor-house and the workhouse
master with his thin gruel and whip, while Christian prelates conduct their worship
at pagan altars.

In his concern for the reinstatement of 'True Principles' Pugin put forward doctrines that were accepted by both 'establishment' theorists at the Schools of Design,
and by the dissenters of the Arts and Crafts movement. Patterns on wallpapers,
he maintained, should be two-dimensional, never shaded: 'Nothing can be more
ridiculous than an apparently reversed groining to walk upon, or highly relieved
foliage and perforated tracery for the decoration of a floor'; ornament should be based
on forms found in nature like 'the finest foliage work in the Gothic buildings' and
when the decoration is two-dimensional 'leaves or flowers [should be] drawn out or
extended, so as to display their geometrical forms'. All ornament should be 'appro-

priate and significant'—there should be no more 'staircase turrets for inkstands, monumental crosses for light-shades, gable ends hung on handles for door-porters, and four doorways and a cluster of pillars to support a French lamp'; the artist, having sought for the most convenient form should then decorate it without concealing 'the real purpose for which the article has been made'.[6]

In spite of his eccentricities and his Roman Catholicism, Pugin's work was in great demand, and his concern for historical authenticity gained him the commission to design the Medieval Court at the Great Exhibition, as well as an extensive practice—he even sent work to America, as he points out in a letter to A. N. Didron.* His authority was recognized by his own generation; Semper paid tribute to him in *Wissenschaft, Industrie und Kunst*, and Matthew Digby Wyatt acknowledged the 'truth and justice of many of his propositions' in the *Journal of Design*.[7] His prestige survived for at least half a century, for although he did not gain the Ruskin seal of approval, the Arts and Crafts generation recognized him as a pioneer in their cause. Voysey praised the integrity which made him more than a mere copyist: 'You may search the Houses of Parliament from top to bottom, and you will not find one superficial yard that is copied from any pre-existing building',[8] and J. D. Sedding told the Art Congress in Liverpool in 1888 that Morris was 'his true lineal descendant. We should have had no Morris, no Street, no Burges, no Shaw, no Webb, no Bodley, no Rossetti, no Burne-Jones, no Crane, but for Pugin.'[9]

Pugin, however, stands firmly in his own generation of design reformers in his attitudes to mechanization. He had none of the Ruskinian loathing of machine processes: his concern was with integrity of design, and he could see no reason why machine techniques, properly applied, should violate that integrity: '. . . in matters purely mechanical' he wrote, 'the Christian architect should gladly avail himself of those improvements and increased facilities that are suggested from time to time. The steam engine is a most valuable power for sawing, raising, and cleansing stone, timber and other materials',[10] and again 'We do not want to arrest the course of inventions, but to confine these inventions to their legitimate uses'.

The 1835 committee

Pugin was not alone in the 1830s and '40s in his concern for design standards, since, on a purely practical level, industrialists and their parliamentary lobby were by that time aware that mechanization was creating aesthetic as well as social problems, and that profit might lie in quality as much as in quantity. One of the first to draw attention to this was, significantly enough, Sir Robert Peel, himself an outstanding representative of the new class, the industrialist, whose fortune was founded on his own, his father's and grandfather's enterprise in developing the Lancashire cotton industry. In April 1832, as Sir Herbert Read pointed out in *Art and Industry*,[11] Peel supported a motion in the House of Commons that a National Gallery should be founded on the

* Reproduced in *Recollections of A. N. W. Pugin*, B. Ferrey, London, 1861, and in *From Gothic Revival to Functional Form*, A. Bøe, Oslo, 1957.

practical, if somewhat misguided, assumption that contemplation of works of art might help to refine the taste of both manufacturers and artisan; he stated as follows:

'. . . motives of public gratification were not the only ones which appealed to the House in this matter; the interest of our manufactures was also involved in every encouragement being held out to the fine arts in this country. It was well known that our manufacturers were, in all matters connected with machinery, superior to all their foreign competitors; but, in pictorial designs, which were so important in recommending the production of industry to the taste of the consumer, they were, unfortunately, not equally successful; and hence they had found themselves unequal to cope with their rivals.' [12]

In the following years it became increasingly obvious that the French, the Belgians and, to a certain extent, the Prussians, were in the possession of that invisible export known as 'taste' which, it seemed, eluded the majority of British manufacturers and which they would obviously have to acquire in order to become fully competitive. In 1835, therefore, three years after the first Reform Bill, a select committee was appointed 'to inquire into the best means of extending a knowledge of the arts and of the principles of design among the people (especially the manufacturing population) of the country'.[13] The chairman was William Ewart, MP for Liverpool, and manufacturers, importers, artists, educationists and members of Parliament were called to give evidence. And although the formation of the committee was to a large extent part of a campaign to undermine the authority of the Royal Academy,[14] this was also the first of a succession of official enquiries aimed at improving standards in industry, and as such it deserves some analysis. For as well as pointing to some of the problems facing the consumer goods industries at that time, the Minutes of Evidence reveal contemporary attitudes to the theory and practice of design and point to the first recognition in Britain of the need for a new kind of specialist, trained to serve industry in a new kind of way.

Much of the evidence, in fact, sounds depressingly familiar. Mr Howell, partner in the 'well known firm of Howell & James, Regent Street' was speaking for many when he declared that he had 'never found a good designer in England', that in 'metallic manufactures the French are vastly superior to the English' and that whereas French manufacturers took the trouble to come over and show him actual samples of the wares they produced, or were hoping to produce, their British counterparts presented him with ill-drawn paper patterns giving little or no indication of the final design. Coade and Seely, it was stated, had formerly employed 'some of the most eminent sculptors, among others, the elder Bacon and Rossi'; Rundell and Bridge (Pugin's patrons) used to employ 'Flaxman, Stothard, Theed and Bailey', but like Wedgwood, they could no longer find artists willing or able to work for them. John Jobson Smith, who manufactured iron stoves in Sheffield, had found a designer, a man of natural talent who had 'studied from nature altogether', whose services were so valuable that he was given 'a share in the business on account of his natural talent'; but like other manufacturers Smith complained of the futility of promoting original work when less scrupulous enterprises copied his designs and undercut his prices. The evidence presented by manufacturers and importers, therefore, all pointed to a dearth of original design talent in Britain, which had led on the one hand to the disreputable practice of copying successful designs, both native and foreign, and on the other, to the need to import at considerable expense, patterns from other countries.

It seemed obvious that England's problem lay to a great extent in an educational system that had ignored the facts of industrial life, and the new demands it had created. Charles Toplis, Vice-President of the London Mechanics' Institute, struck at this fundamental weakness when he maintained that while a privileged few 'waste the whole term of education on the profitless acquisition of the Greek and Latin languages . . . in sterile schemes of tuition calculated merely to rear man for the cloister, the mechanic, the handicraftsman and the peasant found nothing to aid them in their pursuits'.

The Mechanics' Institutes had been founded in 1823, and by 1835 were established in several large cities; their curriculum included 'geometry, mechanical drawing and drawing of ornament, the human figure and landscape', but they were not highly regarded. (In fact in his *True Principles* Pugin had maintained, characteristically, that they were 'a mere device of the day to poison the mind of the operatives with infidel and radical doctrines; the Church is the true mechanic's institute, the oldest and the best. She was the great and never failing school in which all great artists of the days of faith were formed.') Their lack of status, however, was inevitable in a society so schizophrenic in its attitudes to mechanization, so unsure of its definitions of art, and so hidebound in its philosophies of education, at least for the 'humbler' classes. But the fact remains that until 1837 these were the only establishments in Britain which attempted, with any consistency, however pathetic, to teach 'applied' as opposed to 'fine art' to those who might be concerned with industry.

France, as witnesses to the committee were at pains to point out, had, since the days of Colbert, learned how to educate and encourage its artisans and craftsmen; Prussia, too, had established schools of design, and it is significant that the first witness to testify before the select committee was Gustave Waagen, director of the Berlin and Royal Galleries, who was asked to describe the Prussian system of design education. At that time Prussia had five schools serving manufacturing communities in Berlin, Breslau, Königsberg, Danzig and Cologne; the pupils, whose fees were paid by the state, were initially 'instructed in drawing, modelling and perspective', and they then spent two years specializing in a chosen branch of design. None of the students, reported Waagen, had any difficulty in finding employment, and design standards, especially in cotton manufacture, had improved. The whole exercise, implied Waagen, went beyond mere commercial gain: 'the object of the institution is to unite beauty and taste with practability and durability' and to 'restore the happy connection' that existed in the time of Raphael when 'the artists were more workmen and the workmen were more artists'. One of the aims of the Schools of Design, which were established as a result of these investigations, was to restore this 'happy connection'; their concern, to quote the Report of the Committee, which was published in August 1836, was to be 'the direct practical application of the Arts to Manufactures', and their history is linked with the long and generally futile campaign conducted from South Kensington, to marry art and industry. Confidence that such a union could and must be achieved, however, produced several vigorous campaigners in the cause of industrial design, and a design aesthetic that the Arts and Crafts movement was to inherit.

Henry Cole and the Summerly venture

One of the most energetic and, in his own opinion at least, influential of these reformers was Henry Cole, who was associated with most 'official' attempts to improve standards in industry during the 1840s and '50s, and who was to control the Schools of Design for twenty-one years. At the beginning of his two volumes of lengthy reminiscences (*Fifty Years of Public Work of Sir Henry Cole, KCB, accounted for in his deeds, speeches and writings*),[15] Cole supplies a succinct survey of his career and an indication of his industry, eclecticism and self-importance:

'The principal subjects which I now deal with, are the reform of the system of preserving the records of this country . . . my work in expediting the successful introduction of Rowland Hill's Penny Postage; the administration of the Railways; the application of Fine Art to children's books and then to manufactures, which led to the transfer of my duties to the Board of Trade; the Great Exhibition of 1851 and its successors; the Reform of the Patent Laws; the establishment of Schools of Art and Science Classes throughout the United Kingdom; the South Kensington Museum; Drill in Public Elementary Schools as the basis of a National Army, National Training Schools for Music and for Cookery; the Society of Arts and Public Health.'

To all these endeavours he brought the eminently Victorian virtues of diligence and dedication, the ability to rush in where others feared to tread and the enthusiasm of the ambitious amateur. As he indicates in his *curriculum vitae*, his first attempt to extend 'the application of Fine Art' concerned the publication of a series of books for children, and for this enterprise he enlisted the support of 'some of the best modern artists', including Mulready, Cope, Horsley, Redgrave, the Linnells and Townsend.

The success of this venture, and his determination to extend his reforming zeal into new and profitable areas encouraged him to try his hand at designing. In 1846 the Society of Arts offered prizes for the production of 'objects of everyday use', and Cole, using the pseudonym Felix Summerly, submitted a tea-set which he had designed, and which was made by Mintons (pl 4). Cole had spent three days at Mintons 'superintending the throwing, turning and moulding' of the set; as he explained in his autobiography, he wished to produce an article combining 'as much beauty and ornament as is commensurate with cheapness' and he was very concerned with practical qualities, describing how liquid could be poured from the milk jug 'at both angles, right and left, which requires only a motion of the wrist, whilst the usual method needs the lifting of the arm . . .'. The plate, he explained 'is smaller than usual in the rim, because much size in that part is needless'. The tea-set was awarded a silver medal, and it was no doubt this, together with Cole's appointment to the council of the society that same year, which stimulated him to embark on his more elaborate business venture which he called Summerly's Art Manufactures.

He founded the firm in 1847, and, as well as working with some of the artists who had collaborated in the children's book venture, he enlisted the co-operation of Daniel Maclise and John Bell, the sculptor (pls 3, 6 and 7). Several eminent manufacturers including Wedgwoods and Mintons, the Coalbrookdale Company, Hollands the cabinet-makers and Joseph Rodgers, cutlers, promised to produce the work designed by Cole's team.

In this attempt to encourage the liaison between the artist and the manufacturer, Cole was in fact promoting the design ideals that had been tentatively formulated by the select committee, and which had crystallized in the decade following the committee's investigations into a more coherent design philosophy. 'It is the purpose of this collection', wrote Cole, '. . . to revive the good old practice of connecting the best art with familiar objects in daily use. In doing this, Art manufactures will aim to produce in each article superior utility, which is not to be sacrificed to ornament; to select pure forms; to decorate each article with appropriate details relating to its use, and to obtain these details as directly as possible from nature. These principles are by no means put forward as forming a universal rule; but it is thought they may be adhered to advantageously in most articles of use, and may possibly contain the germs of a style which England in the nineteenth century may call its own.' In this short passage Cole sums up the preoccupations of contemporary design theorists. The nostalgia for the good old days, the reference to nature as the source book, the ideal of a native style and the idea that art could and should inspire objects of everyday use had been implicit in attitudes expressed by several witnesses to the select committee. But there was to be one important difference between the Cole group and those who drew their inspiration from Ruskin. Dedicated as they were to the improvement of industrial standards, reformers in the Cole tradition could hardly question the whole basis of nineteenth-century society—theirs was, in theory, a practical rather than a moral approach, and they pursued their goals with optimistic zeal, trusting that a slow process of education for the consumer, manufacturer and designer would eventually have positive results.

In 1849 Cole decided to reinforce his campaign for design reform with the publication of a monthly magazine which he called the *Journal of Design and Manufacture*. Its contributors included Cole's Summerly colleagues, and three important new names: Owen Jones and Matthew Digby Wyatt, who were rapidly establishing themselves as influential critics, and Gottfried Semper, the German exile and architect of the Dresden Opera House. The magazine had, as Cole pointed out in an editorial preface, a 'politics of its own', for like many of its successors in the twentieth century the magazine had a twofold aim. The first was to educate the manufacturer, encourage him to use designers and help him to distinguish between good and bad design, and the second was to press for various reforms that would seem to promote the cause of good design. Among the causes embraced by the *Journal* were the improvement of patent laws, 'a better tribunal to protect copyright in design' and, more significant, the reform of the Schools of Design, which since their foundation in 1837 had been undermined by crises, resignations, insurrections and uncertainty of purpose. Cole was convinced that he and his supporters could manage things better, and that the only way to counter 'the daily growing dissatisfaction of the manufacturers' was to reinforce the original aims of the Schools, establishing a strictly vocational form of training, which would turn out students equipped to meet the needs of industry. The foundation of the *Journal* coincided with Cole's decision to take up the cudgels in the Schools of Design controversy, and the magazine was only continued while it served Cole's purpose. It ceased publication in 1852 when he had successfully lobbied for a select committee to enquire into the affairs of the school and had secured his appointment as secretary and *éminence grise* to the reformed establishment, which was transferred to South Kensington in 1863. He remained in charge until 1873, and although soon after his appointment classes were established in jewellery, metalwork, pottery, woven textiles, furniture and wood-engraving, the stress, during the Cole régime, was on rigidly disciplined drawing rather than on design. The 'cast iron' systems that were associated with the schools' teaching programmes were not intended to produce artists, but they produced neither designers nor technicians; there was little liaison with industry, and Cole's main achievement, according to Ruskin, was to corrupt 'the system of art teaching all over England into a state of abortion and falsehood from which it will take 20 years to recover'.[16]

The Great Exhibition

In 1851, however, Cole was at the height of one of the many pinnacles of his career, for by that time, through his association with the Society of Arts, he had gained the confidence of the reformer royal, the Prince Consort, and had been closely involved in initiating and organizing that shrine (and to some, graveyard) of mid-nineteenth-century design aspirations, The Great Exhibition. This was the first international exhibition ever to be held, and it enabled the British to measure their achievements against those of other nations; but although it provoked a more or less general euphoria, and the conviction, voiced by Prince Albert, that 'Man is approaching a more complete fulfilment of that great and sacred mission which he has to perform in the world', it shocked the design theorists into a new realization of the enormity of the task which faced them. Nearly all the members of the Cole circle were involved, in some capacity, with the exhibition, but although it was to a certain extent their brain-child, they were all unanimous in their condemnation of the exhibits. 'We have no principles', wrote Owen Jones, 'no unity; the architect, the upholsterer, the paper-stainer, the weaver, the calico-printer, and the potter, run each their independent course; each struggles fruitlessly, each produces in art novelty without beauty, or beauty without intelligence.'[17]

Nor were these failings confined to the British exhibits; in the opinion of the critics the exhibition revealed a universal lack of standards. 'The absence of any fixed principles in ornamental design is apparent in the Exhibition', thundered *The Times*, in an article no doubt contributed by a member of the Cole circle (it was reprinted in the *Journal of Design*); '. . . it seems to us that the art manufacturers of the whole of Europe are thoroughly demoralised.'[18] The most powerful weapons, it would seem, to combat this ignorance were education and indoctrination, and following the exhibition the steady stream of books, articles, magazines and pamphlets on the nature of design and ornament swelled into a flood. From the exhibition itself stemmed two English works: Richard Redgrave's *Supplementary Report on Design*, a detailed analysis of the principles of form and ornament and a plea for more logic in the application of decoration, and Matthew Digby Wyatt's magnificent *Industrial Arts of the Nineteenth Century*. Semper's *Wissenschaft, Industrie und Kunst*, prompted by his impressions of the exhibition, was published in German in 1852, and the French report on the exhibition, drawn up by their delegate the Comte de Laborde, was published in Paris in 1856.

These were merely the forerunners; from the South Kensington circle alone came Ralph Wornum's *Analysis of Ornament* in 1856, Richard Redgrave's *Manual of Design*, compiled by his son from his various writings in 1876, and the most impressive and influential of them all, Owen Jones's *Grammar of Ornament* (1856), which by 1910 had been reprinted nine times; Morris undoubtedly used this as a source book, and since an American edition was published in 1880, it can perhaps be assumed that Louis Sullivan was aware of it.[19] These analyses were aimed primarily at the student and potential designer, and the more modest in format were liberally distributed as 'rewards' by the Department of Science and Art. Later in the century successful practitioners such as Lewis Day and Christopher Dresser added to these contributions, bringing their practical experience as designers to their writing.

But this was not all; the manuals and source books were further supplemented by a growing number of magazines. The *Art Union Journal* had been campaigning for design reform since its inception in 1839; on a less exalted level *The Decorator's Assistant* 'a weekly record of Painting, Sculpture and Popular Science' first began publication in 1847, and was succeeded in 1858 by *The Universal Decorator*, a more lavish publication, the aim of which was 'to prove that elaboration of design is not incompatible with the utility of the articles to which it is devoted'. These were directed at the specialist and the practitioner, while the householder was supplied with advice such as that of Sir Charles Eastlake, whose *Hints on Household Taste* was first published in 1868, and whose six New York editions inspired a demand in the States for what was known as 'Eastlake style' furniture, sturdy, simple and faintly rustic.[20]

Publications such as these could not fail to influence the aesthetic assumptions of the Arts and Crafts generation. Their author's aims and the attitudes they expressed were naturally varied, but from them emerged a basic dogma, a royal road for the designer to follow. The designers of the 1880s and '90s who expressed their contempt for South Kensington rigidity, did not entirely reject their tenets but transformed and personalized them in their search for a new humanism of design. For on paper the rules seemed sound. Here, for example, Richard Redgrave in the *Manual of Design*,[21] is analysing the elements of *style*, which he says 'originates in construction, to which decoration is only subsidiary'. After a plea for 'unity of character throughout' he insists 'that the design for a work must have regard to construction, and consequently to proper use of materials', that '*utility* must have precedence of decoration', that 'design must be bad which applies indiscriminately the same constructive forms or ornamental treatment to materials differing in their nature and application', and finally 'that as the greater regulates the lesser, the building should determine the style, and all which it contains of furniture or decoration should conform to its characteristics'.

But in spite of their good intentions, the achievement fell far short of the ideal. In their concern for the rationalization and reform of ornamental principles, these would-be reformers were obsessed not with form, but with decoration; they were further frustrated by an incomplete knowledge of the techniques of manufacture, whether machine or craft-based, and by their inability to establish any valid links with industry. And from 1851 onwards their authority was further undermined by the development of a philosophy of design which denounced their patient negotiations for a marriage between art and industry as misguided and materialist, for as Ruskin was to point out:

'The tap root of all this mischief is in the endeavour to produce some ability in the student to make money by designing for manufacture. No student who makes this his primary object will be able to design at all; and the very words "School of Design" involve the profoundest of art fallacies. Drawing may be taught by tutors, but Design only by Heaven; and to every scholar who thinks to sell his inspiration, Heaven refuses his help.'[22]

2   Ruskin's 'new road'

In 1847 the Lancashire and Yorkshire Mechanics' Institutes invited a distinguished American, Ralph Waldo Emerson, to give a series of lectures, and at a banquet in the Free Trade Hall, Manchester, he duly praised his hosts' 'aristocratic character', which 'in trade and in the mechanics' shop, gives that honesty in performance, that thoroughness and solidity of work, which is a national characteristic'.[1] Ten years later a similar audience in Manchester heard itself admonished rather than praised, for John Ruskin used the occasion of the Art Treasures Exhibition to probe the ethics of work and to remind his listeners of the new responsibilities that wealth had brought them, responsibilities to man, as well as to the art treasures he had created.

It is interesting to compare the attitudes of these two men to art, nature and industry, for they contain the seeds of very divergent national attitudes. Emerson, whose reverence for nature was as profound as that of Ruskin, saw within it organic principles that could be emulated by both art and industry, and in doing so he was blazing the trail that led to Sullivan, Frank Lloyd Wright and Buckminster Fuller. Ruskin, too, urged his followers to turn to nature for both intellectual and emotional stimulus, but for them the field and the factory could have nothing in common, and the lessons they learned from nature bore little relationship to the world of industry: art and craft, in England, was totally divorced from the machine.

Emerson first visited Europe in 1833, touring Sicily, Italy and France before he came to England. In England he met Coleridge, Carlyle and Wordsworth, but he admired that country's ordinary citizens as much as its poets and scholars. His admiration in fact, anticipates that of Loos; the English, he declared, had 'impressed their directness and practical habit on modern civilization'.

'The bias of the nation is a passion for utility. They love the lever, the screw, and pulley, the Flanders draught-horse, the waterfall, wind-mills, tide mills . . . their toys are steam and galvanism. They are heavy at the fine arts, but adroit at the coarse; not good in jewellery or mosaics, but the best iron-masters, colliers, wood-cutters and tanners in Europe. They apply themselves . . . to manufacture of indispensable staples —salt, plumbago, leather, wool, glass, pottery and brick—to bees and silk worms; and by their steady combinations they succeed.'[2]

Before he wrote this, however, Emerson had met, on his first European trip, the American sculptor Horatio Greenough, who was then working in Florence, and whose ideas impressed him profoundly. Greenough, claimed Emerson, in spite of the fact that he was 'a votary of the Greeks, and impatient of Gothic art' had anticipated 'the thoughts of Mr Ruskin as to the *morality* of architecture'[3] and had enthused Emerson with his ideals. 'Here is my theory of structure', he had written in a letter to Emerson: 'A scientific arrangement of spaces and forms to functions and to site; an emphasis of features proportioned to their *gradated* importance in function; colour and ornament to be decided and arranged and varied by strictly organic laws, having a distinct reason for each decision; the entire and immediate banishment of all make-shift and make-believe.'[4]

Greenough achieved contemporary fame with, among other works, his colossal statue of George Washington; his philosophy, summarized in *The Travels, Observations, and Experiences of a Yankee Stonecutter*, which was published in 1852, does not seem to have been widely known, but it is characteristic of the civilization that produced Thoreau and Whitman as well as the architect/philosophers of the twentieth century. For it was Thoreau who maintained that true architecture 'has gradually grown from within outward, out of the character and the necessities of the in-dweller'[5] and it was Greenough, like Frank Lloyd Wright, who urged his compatriots to become 'enamoured of the old, bald, neutral-toned Yankee farmhouse which seems to belong to the ground whereon it stands, as the caterpillar to the leaf that feeds him'[6] and who believed that 'Could we carry into our civil architecture the responsibilities that weigh upon our shipbuilding, we should ere long have edifices as superior to the Parthenon, for the purposes that we require, as the Constitution or the Pennsylvania is to the galley of the Argonauts.'[7]

Had the Industrial Revolution in England produced prophets of functionalism as convincing, eloquent and forceful as an Emerson or a Greenough the retreat to the crafts might never have occurred. But these were representatives of a totally different society, idealists of a New World unfettered by native tradition and culture. Idealists also formed England's attitudes, but England's prophets were unimpressed by the achievement of 'steam and galvanism'; their battle for 'the world of men and life'[8] was a battle against industry and commerce and the values it represented—values that could have no meaning to a vocation as sacred as that of architecture. Here is John Ruskin, in 1857, addressing an audience at the Architectural Association on the *Influence of Imagination in Architecture*:

'Perhaps the first idea which a young architect is apt to be allured by, as a head-problem in these experimental days, is its being incumbent upon him to invent a "new style" worthy of modern civilization in general, and of England in particular; a style worthy of our engines and telegraphs; as expansive as steam, and as sparkling as electricity.'

If this is the case, continues Ruskin, with one of his extraordinary flashes of prophecy: 'You shall draw out your plates of glass and beat out your bars of iron till you have encompassed us all . . . with endless perspective of black skeleton and blinding square . . . you shall put, if you will, all London under one blazing dome of many colours that shall light the clouds round it with its flashing, as far as to the sea. And still, I ask you, what after this?'[9]

Nothing, says Ruskin, nothing but noise, emptiness and idiocy, since such architecture can never be inspired by love—'triple love—for the art which you practise, the creation in which you move, and the creatures to whom you minister'.

It was with an almost priestly sense of vocation and dedication, therefore, that the new generation of architect/craftsmen embarked upon their careers. Their prophet was Ruskin, for it was he, it seemed, who had shaken them awake, provided them with a sense of responsibility and taught them how to see, and judge, the world they lived in.

The true functions of the workman

Ruskin, born in 1819—the same year as Walt Whitman—published his first book, the first volume of *Modern Painters* in 1843; he was still writing *Praeterita* in 1889 when his mind finally collapsed, so that his work spans the second half of the nineteenth century, and his non-stop theorizing (the Cook and Wedderburn edition of his work runs into thirty-nine substantial volumes) both reflects and influenced the preoccupations of four decades. *Modern Painters* was an exercise in art criticism, but Ruskin was incapable of judging art without judging the society that created it, and it was on these foundations that he built a whole structure of social, moral and educational theory. For as he pointed out in the fifth volume of *Modern Painters*:

'In these books of mine, their distinctive character, as essays on art, is their bringing everything to a root in human passion or human hope . . . every principle of painting which I have stated is traced to some vital or spiritual fact; and in my works on architecture, the preference accorded finally to one school over another, is founded on a comparison of their influences on the life of the workman.'[10]

And this, as far as Ruskin was concerned, was the fundamental flaw of the South Kensington circle: their aims were material rather than moral, they looked for rules rather than inspiration, and they attempted to teach design as though it were a branch of manufacture rather than a gift from Heaven. Unlike Morris, Ruskin was not a practising designer, and when he writes about the visual arts, it is painting and architecture that are his primary concerns, and he sees applied design within this wider context. But as with Pugin before him and Morris later, all his assessments are made within a social context; his judgements are concerned first with the nature of men and his personal conception of their needs, and then with the nature of their work, which is only viable when it expresses those needs. The first indication that the art critic was to adopt attitudes that would undermine the patient work of the Cole group appeared in 1849, when Ruskin interrupted his work on *Modern Painters* in order to write *The Seven Lamps of Architecture*, and thus declare his allegiances in the battle of styles. In his first sentence he states his position: 'Architecture is the art which so disposes and adorns the edifices raised by man, for whatsoever uses, that the sight of them may contribute to his mental health, power and pleasure.'

The subsequent chapters, elaborating this conviction that 'Architecture concerns itself only with those characters of an edifice which are above and beyond common use' contain ideas that were to become fundamental to Arts and Crafts theory, even though that theory was to reject Ruskin's distinction between 'mere' building and architecture. 'The Lamp of Truth', for example, is concerned with honesty of expression, material and workmanship; 'architectural deceit', states Ruskin, 'is as truly deserving of reprobation as any other moral delinquency; it is unworthy alike of architecture and of nations'. Deceit, however, does not merely lie in the deplorable practice of imitating stone, marble and alabaster; it can also be found in the quality and quantity of labour:

'For it is not the material, but the absence of human labour, which makes the thing worthless, and a piece of terracotta, or plaster of Paris, which has been wrought by the human hand, is worth all the stone in Carrara cut by machinery. It is, indeed, possible and even usual, for men to sink into machines themselves, so that even hand work has all the character of mechanisation.'

The 'Lamp of Life' elaborates this relationship between man and his work, and by the time Ruskin reaches his final peroration he is defining Arts and Crafts morality:

'We are not sent into this world to do anything into which we cannot put our hearts. We have certain work to do for our bread, and that is to be done strenuously; other work to do for our delight, and that is to be done heartily . . . [But] . . . he who would form the creations of his own mind by any other instrument than his own hand, would also, if he might, give grinding organs to Heaven's angels, to make their music easier. There is dreaming enough, and earthiness enough, and sensuality enough in human existence, without overturning the few glowing moments of it into mechanisation; and since our life must be at best a vapour that appears for a little time and then vanishes away, let it at least appear as a cloud in the height of Heaven, not as the thick darkness that broods over the blast of the Furnace, and rolling of the Wheel.'

Here Ruskin is demonstrating his ability to transcend and transform the conventional attitude. Carlyle before him had condemned a generation that had 'grown mechanical in head and heart, as well as in hand', and had preached salvation through the gospel of work. And this, in spite of Carlyle's criticisms of contemporary society, was a reflection of contemporary opinion, for the sober and prospering middle classes were all too ready to subscribe to the doctrines of self-help, work for the soul's sake and the dignity of labour.* Ruskin also believed in the ethic of work and the dignity of the working class. 'Life without industry is guilt', he was to write; but his corollary 'Industry without art is brutality' marks his divorce from conventional theory, and

---

* 'What can be nobler than industry and work', the Bishop of Oxford had announced in a speech promoting the Great Exhibition. '. . . the exhibition, as promoting the industry of nations, is a great and noble work; it calls attention to the dignity of labour—it sets forth in its true light the dignity of the working class—and it tends to make other people feel the dignity which attaches itself to the producers of these things.'

adds a new dimension to social thinking, for both he and William Morris passionately believed that beauty was as necessary to man's survival as food, shelter and a living wage, and that this essential could only be achieved within a society in which all men would work, take pleasure in their labour and share their delight in its results.

This theme, which was implicit in *The Seven Lamps of Architecture* was elaborated in *The Stones of Venice*, the book that was to form the cornerstone of Arts and Crafts beliefs. The first volume was published in 1851, and the second two in 1853; at least nine selective editions were produced before 1914, each running into several reprints, and it was translated into German at the turn of the century. The book's most significant chapter was, of course, 'On the Nature of Gothic', which forms part of the second volume. This was reprinted as a separate pamphlet and distributed to students at the newly founded Working Men's College, where Ruskin was teaching, in 1854, and a subtitle 'And Herein of the True Functions of the Workman in Art' was added. Morris printed it at the Kelmscott Press in 1892, and wrote in his preface: 'To my mind, and I believe to some others, it is one of the most important things written by the author, and in future days will be considered as one of the very few necessary and inevitable utterances of the century. To some of us when we first read it, now many years ago, it seemed to point out a new road on which the world should travel . . .'

Morris first read the book while he was an undergraduate at Oxford, attempting with his friend Burne-Jones to find in literature and art some basis for a 'crusade and holy warfare against this age'. To these young idealists, and especially to Morris, Ruskin's clarion call had the appeal of total commitment, not only to the ideal of a just society, but to a humanistic aesthetic that would express that society.

Ruskin's argument is based on the theory, already elaborated by Pugin, that Christian architecture is superior to that of the pagan; in elaborating his reasons, however, Ruskin goes further than Pugin, for he insists that architecture and artefacts should unashamedly reveal their man-made origin, and reflect man's essential humanity, with all its roughness and individuality. 'The Greek', according to Ruskin, 'gave to the lower workman no subject which he could not perfectly execute. The Assyrian gave him subjects which he could only execute imperfectly, but fixed a legal standard for his imperfection. The workman was, in both systems, a slave. But in the mediaeval, or especially Christian system of ornament, this slavery is done away with altogether; Christianity having recognised, in small things as well as great, the individual value of every soul. But it not only recognises its value; it confesses its imperfection.'

Perfection of finish, therefore, symmetry and precision, were suspect, since they represented the denial of the human element:

'You are put to a stern choice in this matter. You must either make a tool of the creature, or a man of him. You cannot make both. Men were not intended to work with the accuracy of tools, to be precise and perfect in all their actions. If you would have that precision out of them, and make their fingers measure degrees like cogwheels, and their arms strike curves like compasses, you must unhumanise them.'

Under the present system, says Ruskin, man is forced to be a machine for ten hours a day and humanity is 'saved only by its heart, which cannot go into the form of cogs and compasses, but expands, after the ten hours are over, into fireside humanity'. And it is because men are treated like machines

'. . . that the foundations of society were never yet shaken as they are at this day. It is not that men are ill fed, but that they have no pleasure in the work by which they make their bread, and therefore look to wealth as the only means of pleasure. It is not that men are pained by the scorn of upper classes, but they cannot endure their own; for they feel that the kind of labour to which they are condemned is verily a degrading one, and makes them less than men.'

This demand for individuality rather than standardization, men rather than machines, was to inhibit the campaign for better standards in manufactured goods, for Ruskin's appeal was to the emotions; his attitudes were moral, rather than expedient, and they conflicted with basic assumptions concerning the nature of society:

'We have much studied and much perfected, of late, the great civilised invention of the division of labour; only we give it a false name. It is not, truly speaking, the labour that is divided, but the men:—divided into mere segments of men—broken into small fragments and crumbs of life; so that all the little piece of intelligence that is left in a man is not enough to make a pin, or a nail, but exhausts itself in making the point of a pin, or the head of a nail . . . And the great cry that rises from all our manufacturing cities, louder than their furnace blast, is in all in very deed for this,—that we manufacture everything there except men; we blanch cotton, and strengthen steel, and refine sugar, and shape pottery; but to brighten, to strengthen, to refine, or to form a single living spirit, never enters into our estimate of advantages.'

As Ruskin elaborates his theme he demonstrates how the demand for true dignity of labour will lead to the creation of a new aesthetic. This will involve sacrifice, rather than compromise: 'a determined sacrifice of such convenience, or beauty or cheapness as is to be got only by the degradation of the workman: and by an equally determined demand for the products and results of healthy and ennobling labour'. A just society, says Ruskin, must encourage the efforts of free men, and it can do this by observing 'three broad and simple rules:

'1 Never encourage the manufacture of any article not absolutely necessary, in the production of which *Invention* has no share.
'2 Never demand an exact finish for its own sake, but only for some practical or noble end.
'3 Never encourage imitation or copying of any kind, except for the sake of preserving records of great works.'

It follows, therefore, that it is the product of the creative craftsman that is desirable, rather than that of the factory, and Ruskin demonstrates his argument by insisting on the superiority of Venetian glass to English cut glass.

'Our modern glass is exquisitely clear in its substance, true to its form, accurate in its cutting. We are proud of this. We ought to be ashamed of it. The old Venice glass was muddy, inaccurate in all its forms, and clumsily cut, if at all, and the old Venetian was justly proud of it. For there is this difference between the English and the Venetian workman, that the former thinks only of accurately matching his patterns, and getting his curves perfectly true and his edges perfectly sharp, and becomes a mere machine for rounding curves and sharpening edges, while the old Venetian cared not a whit whether his edges were sharp or not, but he invented a new design for every glass that he made, and never moulded a handle or a tip without a new fancy in it.'

Ruskin made it clear that this plea for roughness and individuality need not imply a loss of standard, but would involve the reinstatement of attitudes to work that, he believed, had prevailed in earlier societies, and that had been lost once the ideal structure of society had been fragmented: 'We want one man to be always thinking, and another to be always working, and we call one a gentleman and the other an operative; whereas the workman ought often to be thinking, and the thinker often to be working, and both should be gentlemen in the best sense.' Such attitudes would abolish the social stigma associated with manual labour, since the professional would become actively involved in his profession: 'The painter should grind his own colours, the architect work in the mason's yard with his men; the master and manufacturer be himself a more skilful operative than any man in the mills; and the distinction between one man and another be only in experience and skill, and the authority and wealth which these must naturally and justly obtain.'

These passages from the 'Nature of Gothic' have been quoted extensively because they provide an obvious guide to the principles on which the Arts and Crafts revival was based. The plea for involvement was the stimulus for work as varied as that of Morris, Mackmurdo, De Morgan, Ashbee and Gimson, and was to lead to the establishment of an aesthetic of individualism which, in fact, had little of the crudity that Ruskin seemed to require. It was also to provide the impetus for a new system of art education, and was to revolutionize the architect's conception of his role in society, culminating in the conviction, expressed by Gropius, that it was the architect's task to bridge 'the disastrous gulf between reality and idealism'.[11]

Involvement

Ruskin himself began to take practical steps to bridge that gulf almost immediately after the publication of *The Stones of Venice*, for in 1854 he agreed to teach at the Working Men's College, which had been founded that year by the Christian Socialist, F. D. Maurice, and which, according to Mackmurdo, who was also to lecture there, 'was one of the first institutions which had for its object the giving to the manual workers some opportunity of satisfying the human instinct for knowledge and beauty. The work carried out there was a real start in the emancipation of the crafts.'[12]

As well as Ruskin, Rossetti, Burne-Jones, Madox Brown, Woolner and Arthur

Hughes were all to teach there, and it is significant that it was this philanthropic institution, rather than the Schools of Design, that aroused their interest and sympathy. This was the first time that Ruskin had had any close contact with the men whose cause he had championed, and he seems to have gained their approval: Madox Brown, for instance, describes going to a meeting to hear 'Professor Maurice and Ruskin spouting, Ruskin was as eloquent as ever, and as wildly popular with the men'.[13] Ruskin published two books in connection with this work—*The Elements of Drawing* (1857) and *The Elements of Perspective* (1859), and this initiation into teaching coincided with his resolve to preach his gospel of responsibility whenever the opportunity arose, as well as to take practical steps to demonstrate the true functions of the workman in art. In 1854, for example, he also became involved in the design and building of Woodward's Oxford Museum, encouraging its builders by insisting that 'nothing was more honorable than a workman in his proper sphere, contributing to the welfare of his fellow men'.[14] Ambitious plans for Rossetti and his friends to embellish the the building proved abortive, although they no doubt inspired the Union Building venture, when William Morris was initiated into the delights and drawbacks of corporate endeavour.

In fact, throughout the 1850s it was becoming increasingly obvious that Ruskin saw himself as a preacher and as a custodian of his country's morals, rather than as an art critic. His view of society was essentially paternalistic; his role at the Working Men's College, as he was to explain, was 'to teach every man to rest contented with his station',[15] but he was also unsparing of his criticisms of those responsible for the education and welfare of the working man. The Manchester 'Art Treasures' lectures[16] have already been mentioned; the audience, no doubt expecting a eulogy on the works of art its enterprise had assembled, were greeted with a carefully argued discourse on the duties of a state and its citizens. The state, maintained Ruskin, should be run like a well-ordered household, each individual contributing to the well-being of the whole, the young being educated in skills fitting to their station, and the old protected, rather than cast aside, when they had outgrown their usefulness. Similarly it was the duty of the state to protect, encourage and nurture artistic talent, for its wealth should be measured, not by its material achievement but in terms of human happiness, and by the works of art it produces. It was in this book, too, that Ruskin first put forward the idea that the government should ensure basic standards of workmanship; he urged, for example, that the state should establish paper and colour factories, thus guaranteeing its artists a certain standard of quality, and he also recommended the re-establishment of the guild system as a means of controlling unemployment and maintaining standards of workmanship—a theme that was to be taken up by Mackmurdo, Ashbee and Lethaby.

Whatever the occasion, Ruskin treated his audience to unorthodox opinions. In his address on *Modern Manufacture and Design*, for example, which inaugurated the new school of design in Bradford in 1859, he attacked one of the premises of teaching in such schools—namely that designers should not be taught life drawing. 'The fact is, that all good subordinate forms of ornamentation ever yet existent in the world have been invented, and others as beautiful *can* only be invented, by men primarily exercised in drawing or carving the human figure.'[17] He also informed the industrialists present that their 'business, as manufacturers, is to form the market, as much as to supply it'; he urged them to surround their men 'with happy influences and beautiful things' and produce 'work substantial rather than rich in make; refined rather than splendid in design . . . such as may at once serve the need and refine the taste, of a cottager'. (Undaunted, the citizens of Bradford were later to invite Ruskin to lecture to them on the architecture appropriate to the new Exchange they were planning: 'If', said Ruskin, 'you chose to . . . do your commerce, and your feeding of nations, for fixed salaries; and to be as particular about giving people the best food, and the best cloth, as soldiers are about giving them the best gunpowder, I could carve something for you or your Exchange worth looking at. But I can only at present suggest decorating its frieze with pendant purses; and making its pillars broad at the base, for the sticking of bills.')[18]

Until 1860 Ruskin's forays into social criticism were greeted with either indulgence or indifference—the permitted eccentricities of a man who wrote and spoke so eloquently about art. In 1860, however, Ruskin went beyond the bounds of decency, and in a series of articles written for the new magazine *Cornhill*, launched a bitter attack on the current industrial system, with an indictment of the *laissez-faire* economy on which it was based. These articles, which were published in 1862 as *Unto This Last*, are in effect an elaboration of the ideas on political economy which Ruskin had already put forward in *The Political Economy of Art* and *The Two Paths*. The argument was based on what Ruskin called 'the great, palpable, inevitable fact, the rule and root of all economy', namely 'that what one person has, another cannot have', and in declaring this, Ruskin was, in effect, declaring war on the sacred laws of supply and demand. His description of the attributes of the rich and the poor in such an economy, was unorthodox, to say the least, to nineteenth-century ears:

'. . . in a community regulated only by laws of demand and supply, but protected from open violence, the persons who became rich are, generally speaking, industrious, resolute, proud, covetous, prompt, methodical, unimaginative, insensitive and ignorant. The persons who remain poor are the entirely foolish, the entirely wise, the idle, the reckless, the humble, the thoughtful, the dull, the imaginative, the sensitive, the well-informed, the improvident, the irregularly and impulsively wicked, the clumsy knave, the open thief, and the entirely merciful, just and godly person.'

Even more incomprehensible, and thus unforgivable, was Ruskin's indictment of the rich who 'not only refuse food to the poor; they refuse wisdom; they refuse virtue, they refuse salvation'. To replace this economy of grab and gain Ruskin envisaged a system that would provide free education for the young, with housing and security for the old, handicapped and destitute. The old guild system would be replaced by schemes of vocational training in government workshops, which would maintain standards of work, workmanship and payment; the unemployed could be directed to these workshops or to public works, and within such a fairly ordered society such concepts as a minimum wage, fair rents and a ceiling on incomes could also be considered. The reaction to this embryonic ideal of the welfare state was immediate and violent. 'If we do not crush him', said the *Manchester Examiner and Times*, 'his wild words will touch the springs of action in some hearts, and before we are aware, a moral floodgate may fly open and drown us all.'[19]

The *Saturday Review* dismissed Ruskin's reasoning as 'eruptions of windy hysterics' and 'intolerable twaddle' and declared that the world was not going to be 'preached to death by a mad governess'.[20] Only Carlyle, it seemed, approved of these heretical demands for state interference: 'I have read your paper with exhilaration, exultation, often with laughter, with bravissimo!' he wrote to Ruskin.[21] The immediate result was that Thackeray, the editor of *Cornhill*, was forced to abandon the series: 'the papers', he said, 'seem to be too deeply tainted with socialistic heresy to conciliate the subscribers'. On a more profound level, however, the furore seems to have convinced Ruskin at least temporarily, that, until a new basis of social order could be established, his preoccupation with aesthetic values was a waste of time. In 1865, in an address to the Institute of British Architects he stated: 'For my own part I feel the force of mechanisation and the fury of avaricious commerce to be at present so irresistible, that I have seceded from study, not only of architecture, but nearly of all art; and have given myself, as I would in a besieged city, to seek the best modes of getting bread and butter for its multitudes.'[22] One of the practical steps he took was to refuse to have any of his books on art reprinted in an endeavour to concentrate attention on his social theories; and it was about this time (1864) that he provided Octavia Hill with the funds to renovate 'three houses in one of the worst courts in Marylebone'. Many of Ruskin's practical attempts at reform, however, were tinged with the impractical, especially in the 1870s, when his mental breakdowns were becoming more frequent and more severe. His most ludicrous effort was the enlistment of undergraduates to build a road at Hinksey during his Slade Professorship at Oxford, and the most Utopian was his ideal for the St George's Guild, a scheme which preoccupied him from 1871 when he began to publish *Fors Clavigera* in the form of *Letters to the Workmen and Labourers of Gt. Britain*.

The St George's Guild

This enterprise was directed towards the achievement of both moral and economic reform, and unlike the various arts and crafts guilds founded in the 1880s, was not directly concerned with the extension of craft techniques. It was Ruskin's aim, by means of the Guild, to put his ideal of a just society into practice. The idea was to establish communes of like-minded men, drawn from all ranks of society, whose way of life, simple and dedicated to the basic human values, would so commend itself that a new social order, in essence a kind of enlightened feudalism, would permeate not only the British Isles but every society crippled by the canker of capitalism.

In order to establish the first communes, Ruskin set up a fund, to which, it was sug-

1 Silk brocatelle, designed by A. W. N. Pugin for F. Crace & Son, *c.* 1850 *Victoria and Albert Museum*

2 Necklace and cross in enamelled gold, set with garnets and pearls. Designed by A. W. N. Pugin for John Hardman & Co., 1848-50 *Victoria and Albert Museum*

3 Water carafe, enamelled and gilt; designed by Richard Redgrave and made for Summerly's Art Manufactures by J. F. Christy, 1847 *Victoria and Albert Museum*

4 Tea service designed by Henry Cole (using the pseudonym Felix Summerly) and made by Mintons. The service was awarded a silver medal by the Society of Arts in 1847 *Victoria and Albert Museum*

5 Silver teapot, designed by John Hardman Powell (a pupil of Pugin) for John Hardman & Co., Birmingham, 1861-2. Shown at the International Exhibition, 1862 *Victoria and Albert Museum*

6 A set of silver decanter stoppers in the form of Bacchanalian boys; designed by J. C. Horsley for Summerly's Art Manufactures, and made by Benjamin Smith, jr *Victoria and Albert Museum*

7 Paper knife (left) and bread knife (right) designed by John Bell for Summerly's Art Manufactures. The paper knife has a gilt metal blade and carved ivory handle; the blade of the bread knife is engraved with the name of the manufacturer (Joseph Rodgers & Sons) and designer; its handle is in carved boxwood *Victoria and Albert Museum*

opposite
8 Cabinet designed by Gottfried Semper, and made by Holland & Sons, 1855. Ebony, with gilt metal mounts; the plaques are by Wedgwood, and the porcelain panel is painted with a copy of Mulready's *Crossing the Brook. Victoria and Albert Museum*

9 *Iris Florentina;* pencil and watercolour by John Ruskin, 1871
Ashmolean Museum, Oxford

9

10

10 *John Ruskin;* portrait by J. E.
Millais, 1854. *Coll. Mrs. Patrick
Gibson.* Photo: *Royal Academy*

opposite
11 *Moss and wild strawberry:* pencil and
watercolour by John Ruskin, 1880
Ashmolean Museum, Oxford

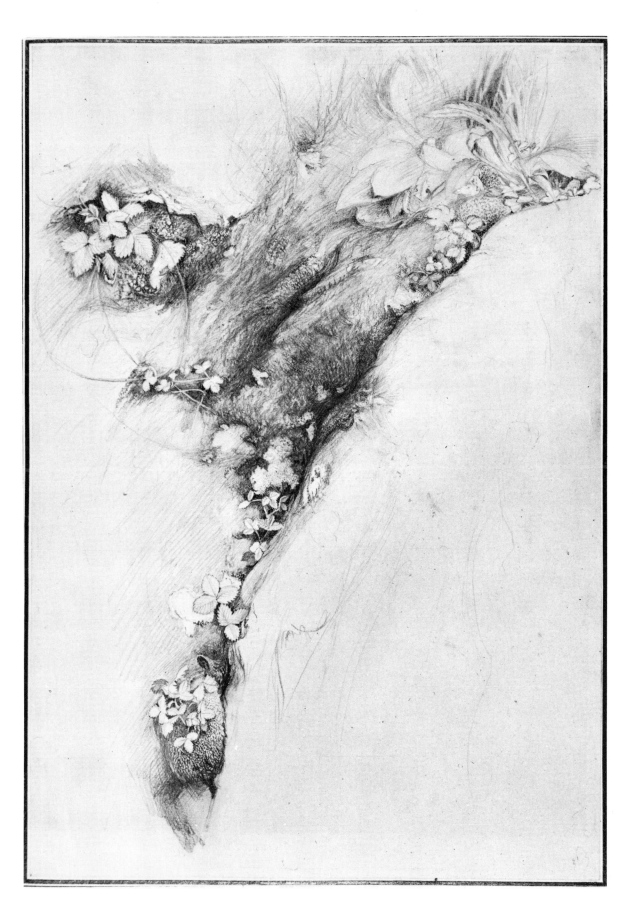

12

12 William Morris *William Morris Gallery, Waltham-stow, Essex*

13 One of a pair of copper candlesticks, designed by Philip Webb for Burne-Jones, *c.* 1861 *Victoria and Albert Museum*

14 One of a group of glasses designed by Philip Webb in 1859, and made by J. Powell & Sons, White-friars. Probably exhibited by Morris, Marshall, Faulkner & Co., at the International Exhibition of 1862 *Victoria and Albert Museum*

13

14

15 Embroidery designed by William Morris *c.* 1880 *Victoria and Albert Museum*

16 *Beauty and the Beast:* earthenware tile panel painted with six scenes designed by Edward Burne-Jones; blue and white painted repeat pattern surround. Produced as an overmantle for Birket Foster's house at Witley, Surrey, 1862 *William Morris Gallery, Walthamstow, Essex.* Photo: *Peter Hirst-Smith*

15

16

How a Prince who by enchantment was under the form of a beast became a man again by the love of a certe in maiden

17 Furniture designed by Ford Madox Brown and made by Morris & Co. from the early 1860s *Society of Antiquaries.* Photo: *Peter Locke*

18 St George's cabinet; mahogany and pinewood. Designed by Philip Webb and painted by William Morris with scenes from the legend of St George, 1861 *Victoria and Albert Museum*

19 Sideboard painted by Edward Burne-Jones. Oil on wood, 1860 *Victoria and Albert Museum*

opposite
20 Morris's bedroom at Kelmscott Manor; the Elizabethan four-poster bed has embroideries by Janey and May Morris *Society of Antiquaries*. Photo: *A. F. Kersting*

21 Rosewood cabinet inlaid with purple wood and ebony: mounts in 'oldsilver'. Designed by W. A. S. Benson and made by Morris & Co., *c.* 1899 *Victoria and Albert Museum*

22 Chair, based on traditional Sussex
design and produced by Morris, Marshall, Faulkner & Co., from 1865.
Morris's *Fruit* or *Pomegranate* wallpaper, designed in 1864, is in the
background; the *Lily* carpet is a
machine-made Wilton *Victoria and
Albert Museum*

23 Rush-seated chair; turned wood
painted black. Based on a traditional
Sussex design and made by Morris,
Marshall, Faulkner & Co., in the
1870s *Victoria and Albert Museum*

24 An oak armchair with rush seat; probably designed in Norman Shaw's office in 1876 and sold by Morris & Co. *Victoria and Albert Museum*

25 Mahogany armchair with cane back and sides; made by Morris & Co., in 1893. Cushion covered with *Tulip* chintz, designed in 1875 *Victoria and Albert Museum*

26 A. H. Mackmurdo *William Morris Gallery, Walthamstow, Essex*

27 Dining chair, designed by A. H. Mackmurdo for the Century Guild, 1882-3; made by Collinson and Lock. The chair has a mahogany frame and upholstered seat; the swirling stem and flower forms in the fretwork back (see also pl. 30) recall the title page for *Wren's City Churches William Morris Gallery, Walthamstow, Essex*. Photo: *Peter Hirst-Smith*

opposite
28 Cabinet designed by A. H. Mackmurdo, and made by E. Goodall of Manchester *c*. 1886, possibly for Pownall Hall. Satin-wood and mahogany with brass fittings. The quotation is from Shelley *William Morris Gallery, Walthamstow, Essex*. Photo: *Peter Hirst-Smith*

29 Clock, probably designed by Herbert Horne; mahogany, painted with Roman numerals and signs of the Zodiac. The clock's fingers are missing *William Morris Gallery, Walthamstow, Essex*. Photo: *Peter Hirst-Smith*

30 Mahogany framed wall-mirror, with a glove compartment and the characteristic fretwork at the base *William Morris Gallery, Walthamstow, Essex*

31 Title page from Mackmurdo's *Wren's City Churches*, published by G. Allen, Orpington, Kent, in 1883; the book was printed on hand-made paper *William Morris Gallery, Walthamstow, Essex*

32 Title page of the *Hobby Horse*, designed by Selwyn Image. *Hobby Horse* was first published in 1884; it had wood-cut illustrations by Image and Herbert Horne, and was printed on hand-made paper *William Morris Gallery, Walthamstow, Essex*

opposite
34 *Floral design*, cut velvet; designed by A. H. Mackmurdo *William Morris Gallery, Walthamstow, Essex*. Photo: *Peter Hirst-Smith*

opposite
35 *Queen Summer* or *Tourney of the Lily and the Rose*; illustrated by Walter Crane, and published by Cassell & Co. 1891 *William Morris Gallery, Walthamstow, Essex*. Photo: *Peter Hirst-Smith*

33 *The Story of the Glittering Plain*; printed at the Kelmscott Press, 1894. *Chaucer* type with twenty-three wood-cuts designed by Walter Crane and cut by A. Leverett *William Morris Gallery, Walthamstow, Essex*. Photo: *Peter Hirst-Smith*

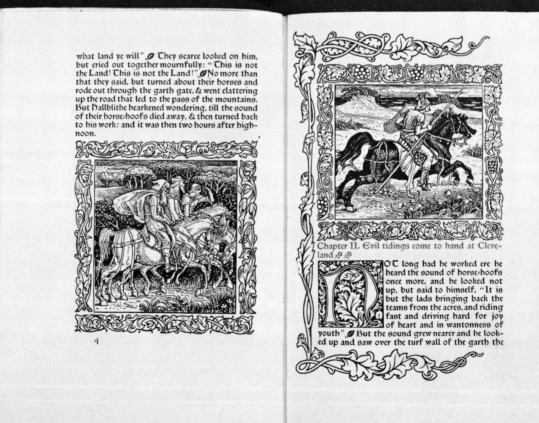

34

35

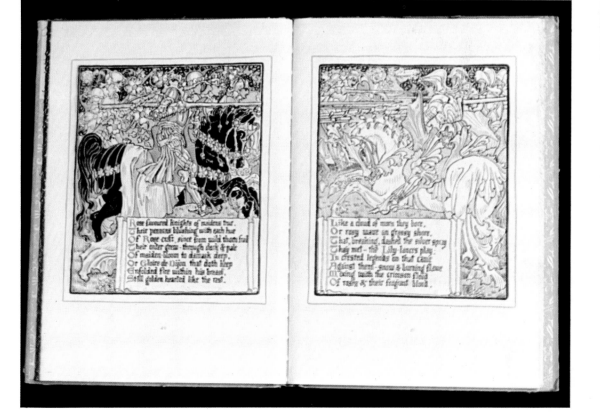

36 *Single flower*, cretonne, designed by A. H. Mackmurdo *c.* 1882, and printed by Simpson & Godlee in various colourways *William Morris Gallery, Walthamstow, Essex*

37 *Peacock*, cretonne, designed by A. H. Mackmurdo, and printed by Simpson & Godlee *c.* 1882 *William Morris Gallery, Walthamstow, Essex*

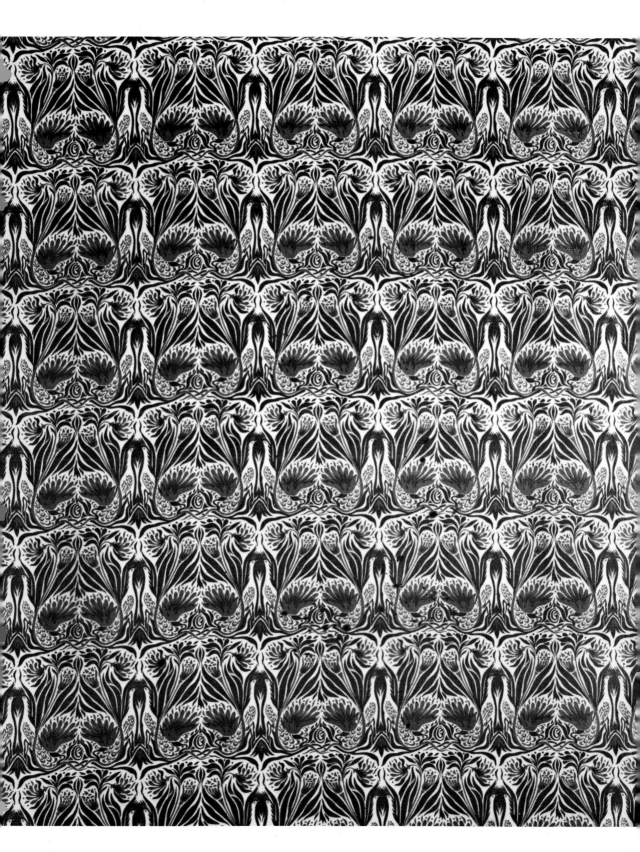

a

b

c

d

38 Pownall Hall in Cheshire was restored for its owner, Henry Boddington, in 1886 and the Century Guild was commissioned to undertake part of this work

a Front door, decorated with iron work by the Guild

b Detail of the knocker in the form of a winged dragon

c Detail of one of two brass sconces on either side of the fireplace in the Pownall Hall entrance hall; the sconces, which are hammered and pierced with small holes, were evidently used for gas lighting at some stage

d Circular brass dish with relief decoration made by George Esling for the Century Guild in 1883. Diameter 1 ft 8 ins *Colchester and Essex Museum*

e Cast brass lamp standard designed by A. H. Mackmurdo in 1884, and made by George Esling, a Century Guild metalworker. Height 17 ins; diameter 10½ ins (this may also have been used as a *jardinière*) *Colchester and Essex Museum*

f Sconce in repoussé copper designed by A. H. Mackmurdo in 1884, and made by Kellock Brown, one of the metalworkers associated with the Century Guild *Colchester and Essex Museum*

g Mahogany and satinwood box with brass hinges designed by A. H. Mackmurdo in 1884; the inlay, which was designed by Selwyn Image, is similar to that on a small table in the possession of the William Morris Gallery *Colchester and Essex Museum*

e

f

g

39 *The Trades*, part of a set of twelve tiles designed by J. Moyr Smith for Mintons *c.* 1880. These designs also appeared on Minton plates. *William Morris Gallery, Walthamstow Essex.* Photo: *Peter Hirst-Smith*

40 Illustration of Howell & James' paintings on porcelain, reproduced from the *Art Journal* catalogue of the Paris International Exhibition, 1878

PARIS INTERNATIONAL EXHIBITION.

The engravings on this page are selected from the very large collection of Paintings on Porcelain exhibited by Messrs. HOWELL and JAMES in Paris, and now shown at their galleries in Regent Street. They are chiefly the works of amateurs, sent in response to the offer of prizes in competition; but many of them would do credit to the most accomplished professors of the art. It was a happy idea, that which directed the attention of ladies to an employment at once pleasant and remunerative, giving, or rather extending, occupation for women — a social requirement universally admitted. We engrave on this page five of the works.

Nos. 1 and 3, two plaques by Miss Kelly, were purchased by the Prince of Wales; No. 2 is by Mrs. Nesbitt, some of whose works her Majesty has commissioned; No. 4 is by Mrs.

Sparkes, also purchased by the Prince of Wales; and No. 5 is a portrait of Lady Eva Greville, by her mother, the Countess of Warwick, to which was awarded the Gold Medal presented by her Imperial Highness the Crown Princess of Germany.

41 Cabinet; ebonized and gilt, inlaid with plaques of stoneware made by Doulton & Co.; shown at the International Exhibition, 1872 *Victoria and Albert Museum*

42 Stoneware vase with incised dragon devices, inscribed R. W. Martin Bros, London, Southall, 1888 *Ernest Marsh Collection, Kingston-upon-Thames Museum.* Photo: *Peter Hirst-Smith*

43 Brown saltglazed stoneware pot with scale design, 1884; inscribed Martin Bros, London & Southall, 10-84 *Ernest Marsh Collection, Kingston-upon-Thames Museum.* Photo: *Peter Hirst-Smith*

44 Wall plaque; the plinth is supported by oak leaves and a terminal in the form of a grotesque head. The Martin brothers produced several of the plaques, which recall the fact that Wallace worked on the decoration of the Houses of Parliament after Pugin's death. *Ernest Marsh Collection, Kingston-upon-Thames Museum.* Photo: *Peter Hirst-Smith*

45 Walter (left), Wallace (centre) and Edwin Martin photographed in their studio at Southall in 1910. Photograph from the *Nettlefold Catalogue*

46 Glass claret jug with silver mount, designed by Christopher Dresser, 1879-80 *Victoria and Albert Museum*

47 Two vases of 'Clutha' glass, designed by Christopher Dresser and made by James Couper & Son, Glasgow, *c.* 1880 *Victoria and Albert Museum*

48 Earthenware dish with painted decoration, designed by Lewis F. Day, 1877 *Victoria and Albert Museum*

49 William De Morgan: Portrait sketch in coloured chalks by his wife, Evelyn De Morgan, 1907

50 Six-inch tile designed by William De Morgan: yellow flower and green leaves on a white ground. Similar tiles made in two-toned blue and red

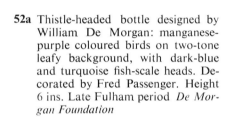

53 Top: five panels of sixty six-inch tiles designed by William De Morgan, decorated with flower and frond design in Persian colours. Fireplace panels decorated with carnation arabesque design in Persian colours *The Richmond Fellowship*

54a A fourteen-inch plate designed by William De Morgan with two squirrels in iron red on a background of yellow lustre trees with fruit. Decorated by Charles Passenger. Fulham Period *The De Morgan Foundation*

54b Deep dish, belonging to William De Morgan's 'Sunset and Moonlight Suite', triple lustred in copper, silver and gold, with design in turquoise and deep lapis-lazuli on a mixed cobalt and manganese-purple ground. Decorated by Charles Passenger. Painted mark CP. Diameter 11¾ ins. Late Fulham Period *Coll. M. D. E. Clayton-Stamm*

opposite
55 Stoneware bird figure with detachable head; probably used as a tobacco jar; modelled by Wallace Martin, *c.* 1899 and inscribed Martin Bros, London & Southall *Ernest Marsh Collection, Kingston-upon-Thames Museum.* Photo: *Peter Hirst-Smith*

56 Stoneware teapot inscribed Martin Bros, London & Southall *Ernest Marsh Collection, Kingston-upon-Thames.* Photo: *Peter Hirst-Smith*

58 Cabinet in brown ebony, inlaid with mother-of-pearl; designed by Ernest Gimson in 1908
Leicester Museum and Art Gallery

57 Cabinet in English walnut, inlaid with darker walnut and cherry with hand-made brass handles; designed by Ernest Gimson and made by Peter Waals

59 Inlaid walnut cabinet designed by Ernest Gimson and made in the Daneway workshops. It is one of Gimson's last designs

opposite
61 Ladder-backed chair designed and made by Ernest Gimson *Leicester Museum and Art Gallery*

60 Dining table in English walnut, designed by Ernest Gimson and made by H. Davoll in the Daneway workshops

63 Silver cupboard in figured walnut, designed and made by Peter Waals, 1925 *Victoria and Albert Museum*

62 Walnut sideboard with brass handles; wrought-iron candle sticks and a walnut box all designed by Ernest Gimson. The sideboard was made by H. Davoll at the Daneway workshop

64 Silk tissue, designed by Owen Jones and woven by Benjamin Warner, Spitalfields, 1870-80 *Victoria and Albert Museum*

66 *The Owl*, woollen cloth tissue, designed by C. F. A. Voysey, for A. Morton & Co, 1897. *Victoria and Albert Museum*

67 Silk and wool-cloth; designed by C. F. A. Voysey, for A. Morton & Co., 1897. *Victoria and Albert Museum*

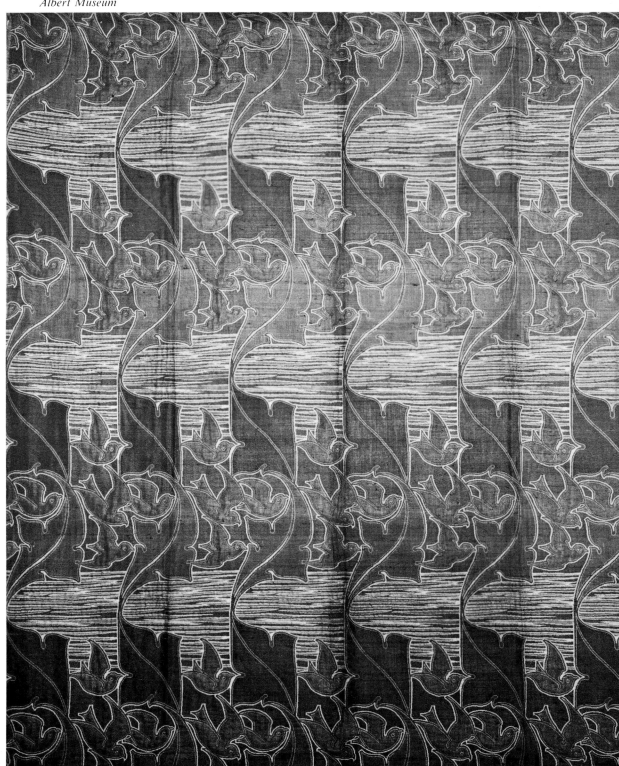

opposite

68 Oil lamp in cast and turned brass and copper, designed *c.* 1890 by W. A. S. Benson. It comes from Standen, East Grinstead, Sussex (designed by Philip Webb in 1891) and was sold by Morris & Co. *Victoria and Albert Museum*

69 Bronze and copper candelabra, designed and made by W. A. S. Benson, and bought for Wightwick Manor, by Mrs. Joseph (*née* Gladys Holman Hunt). In the background, Morris's *Peacock and Dragon* fabric; the plaster ceiling is by L. A. Shuffrey. *National Trust.* Photo: *Colin Bailey*

70 Range of hollow-ware designed and made by W. A. S. Benson. From left to right: silver-plated nickel coffee pot with cane-covered handle and wooden knob, *c.* 1910; silver-plated milk jug, 1910; copper and nickel teapot, with spun body and turned spout, 1895-1900 *Victoria and Albert Museum*

69

70

72 Kettle, stand and spirit burner in silver-plated copper. Designed by Arthur Dixon for the Birmingham Guild of Handicraft, 1905-10. *Victoria and Albert Museum*

71 Silver gilt flagon designed for Gloucester Cathedral by J. D. Sedding and made by F. Courthorpe in 1891. The inscription reads 'in memoriam Richard and Eliz Harvey' and the gadrooned cover is surmounted by the Pelican in her Piety. *The Worshipful Company of Goldsmiths*

73 Two jugs in copper and brass, designed by Arthur Dixon for the Birmingham Guild of Handicraft, *c.* 1895. *Victoria and Albert Museum*

74 Silver vase with marble stand, designed and made by Omar Ramsden and Alwyn Carr. London hallmark for 1900-1. *Victoria and Albert Museum*

75 Pendant necklace; silver open-work, set with mother-of-pearl and emeralds. Designed and made by Mr & Mrs Arthur Gaskin, Birmingham *c.* 1912 *Victoria and Albert Museum*

76 Picture panel composed of three six-inch tiles decorated with fantastic bird in polychrome colours. Designed by William De Morgan and painted by D. and F. Sirocchi. Fulham period *Col. M. D. E. Clayton-Stamm*

77 Dish with serpent and sunflower motif in raised relief against exotic foliage. Designed by William De Morgan and decorated by Charles Passenger. Painted mark CP. Diameter 14ins. Fulham period *De Morgan Foundation*

gested, well-wishers should devote one-tenth of their income. The money donated was to be used to buy land, which was to be cultivated as far as possible, by manual labour. 'It is to be carefully noted', wrote Ruskin, 'that *machinery* is only forbidden by the guild where it supersedes healthy bodily exercise, or the art and precision of manual labour in decorative work: but that the only permitted *motive power* of machining is by natural force of wind or water (electricity perhaps not in future refused); but *steam* is absolutely refused, as a cruel and furious waste of fuel to do what every stream and breeze are ready to do costlessly . . . gunpowder and steam hammers are today the toys of the insane and the paralytic.'[23] Wise overseers were to be put in charge of each community and as land was donated or acquired, new cottages were to be built or existing ones renovated; schools were to established, where the Ruskinian ideals of education were to be pursued, but the priority—the whole object of these exercises—was to be the wise cultivation of the land, since true human values were to be found in the fields rather than the factories. The *Fors* letters were used to state the objectives and report progress, and letter 17 (1872) summarizes the duties of the guildsmen:

'. . . they are to be entirely devoted, according to their power, first to the manual labour of cultivating pure land, and guiding pure streams and rains to the places where they are needed; and secondly, together with this manual labour and much by its means, they are to carry on the thoughtful labour of true education, in themselves, and of others. And they are not to be monks or nuns, but are to learn, and teach all fair arts, and the sweet order and obedience of life; and to educate the children entrusted to their schools in such practical arts and patient obedience, but not at all necessarily in either arithmetic, writing or reading.'[24]

Such then were the ideals; the reality of course fell far short of them. Ruskin launched his scheme in 1871 and inaugurated the fund with a personal donation of £7000. By 1874 he had collected a mere £200, and in 1875 the guild received its first donation of land—3 acres of moorland in Barmouth, with eight delapidated cottages. Two years later the guild embarked on its most ambitious venture—the acquisition of some 14 acres in Sheffield to enable a group of self styled 'communists' to found a community along Ruskinian lines. The group were not guild members, but Ruskin offered advice and enthusiasm, as well as patronage, because: 'Sheffield is in Yorkshire, and Yorkshire is yet in the main temper of its inhabitants Old English, and capable, therefore, yet of the idea of honesty and piety by which old England lived: finally because Sheffield is within easy reach of beautiful natural scenery.'[25] Predictably enough, in spite of Yorkshire spirit and idyllic scenery, the scheme failed, and the community, frustrated in its brave plans to grow strawberries and gooseberries on the bleak acres, dispersed. One concrete memorial to Ruskin, however, remained—the Ruskin Museum, which he opened in 1875. The collection, carefully assembled by Ruskin for the edification and delight of local labourers and schoolchildren, consisted of paintings, sculpture, prints, casts and specimens, and remained in Sheffield until the 1950s when the bulk of it was acquired by Reading University.

Subsequent experiments were equally abortive, and Ruskin's editors provided a gloomy, if accurate summary of the guild's achievements when they stated that it consisted of a 'Master, who, when wanted to discuss legal deeds, was often drawing leaves of *anagallis tenella*; a society of companions, few and influential; some cottages in Wales; twenty acres of partly cleared woodland in Worcestershire; a few bleak acres in Yorkshire, and a single museum.'[26]

Ruskin, however, must be judged as a philosopher and visionary, rather than as a man of action, and it was not the doubtful achievement but the idealism that inspired it that was to have so profound an influence on social thinking, as well as on attitudes to design and architecture. Ruskin was a strange compound of the radical and the reactionary, and his followers found within his convictions and inconsistencies, his flights of fancy and his sound sense of social priorities, theories that matched their own aspirations. By 1910, for example, *Unto This Last* had been translated into French, German, Italian and Gujurati: 'That book', said Gandhi, 'was the turning point of my life.'[27] It was also cited by the Labour MPs returned to Parliament in 1906 as the work that had most profoundly influenced them.

But, as Morris was to complain, few of Britain's early Socialists were to recognize the ideal of art and craftsmanship as a redemptive force in modern life—their weapons were trade unions, not guilds—and they were in effect discounting the one firm conviction on which all Ruskin's premises were based. Nevertheless, Ruskin had, through a lifetime of teaching and preaching, succeeded in establishing the idea of design and architecture as the expression of a way of life. He was himself clear about the form that life should take—given the opportunity, men could be happy, orderly and good, and given the opportunity, a system of architecture would arise to express that harmony; such an architecture would not be based on imitation of past achievements, nor would it reflect present conflicts: 'We don't want either the life or the decorations of the thirteenth century back again', he told the manufacturers at the School of Design at Bradford,[28] 'and the circumstances with which you must surround your workmen are those simply of happy modern English life, because the designs you have now to ask for from your workmen are such as will make modern English life beautiful'; the industrialist, faced with a decision whether to 'make his wares educational instruments, or mere drugs on the market', was urged to produce what is best, 'on an intelligent consideration of the probable tendencies and possible tastes of the people whom you supply'.

Ruskin, of course, was convinced of the innate goodness of man. His first sermon, to his father's household at the age of five, was 'People, be good', and he preached a variation of this message throughout his life. The theme was Utopian, but it was one that was to influence attitudes to design and architecture for well over a century, and the belief that a better environment will produce better men is still with us today. Now, however, it seems a matter of survival rather than morality.

Ruskin's disciples within the Arts and Crafts movement were but children when he was grappling with his problems of conscience and commitment, and many of them lived well into the twentieth century. Mackmurdo, for example, was born in 1851; twenty years later and inspired by *Fors Clavigera* he met the master and travelled with him to Italy; he founded the Century Guild in 1882, and survived until 1942. Ashbee, who was twelve years younger than Mackmurdo, also died in 1942, and Lethaby, founder of the London Central School of Arts and Crafts, died in 1931. This generation of craftsmen, architects and teachers inherited Ruskin's idealism, but they did not share his sense of isolation.

In the 1860s and '70s Ruskin seemed, both by temperament and circumstances, a voice crying in the wilderness; he could, according to Madox Brown, be 'playful and childish'[29] with the young Pre-Raphaelites, plying them with cakes, but he attracted pupils and admirers, rather than friends. The generation that was active in the 1880s and 1890s, however, no longer felt themselves men apart. They belonged to a body of professionals who had specific objectives and a clearly defined context within which to apply them. The objectives had been defined both by Ruskin and by those working for better standards in industry, and aspects of both ideologies contributed to Arts and Crafts thinking. Some twenty years after Ruskin had uttered his heresies in *Cornhill* and South Kensington had organized its second International Exhibition, design and architecture had become a career for the committed, and the man who did most to establish England's reputation as a nation of dedicated designers was William Morris.

3 Theory into practice: William Morris

In 1860, when Ruskin was wrestling with *Unto This Last*, Morris was moving with his new bride into the Red House, and having attempted a career first in architecture and then in painting, was about to set himself up as a 'decorator'. Because of its associations with Morris and his Firm, the Red House ('more a poem than a house', according to Rossetti)[1] is considered something of a landmark in nineteenth-century domestic architecture. Morris, however, was himself aware of the various influences that conditioned his requirements, and Webb's interpretation of them. Giving an account of his life in 1883,[2] he described his apprenticeship to Street and his friendship with Rossetti, and continues 'At this time the revival of gothic architecture was making great progress in England and naturally touched the Pre-Raphaelite movement also; I threw myself into these movements with all my heart; got a friend to build me a house very mediaeval in spirit in which I lived for five years, and set myself to decorating it.'

The house, then, was to be the realization, in red bricks and mortar, of a vision of the ideal life that Morris and his friends had constructed for themselves at Oxford and in London. Foremost among these friends was Edward Burne-Jones who, like Morris, went up to Exeter College in January 1853; Burne-Jones was from Birmingham, and both he and Morris felt themselves isolated from their contemporaries:

'The place was languid and indifferent . . . so we compared our thoughts together upon these things and went angry walks together in the afternoons and sat together in the evenings reading . . . Before many weeks were past in our first term there were but three or four men in the whole college whom we visited or spoke to. But at Pembroke there was a little Birmingham colony and with them we consorted when we wanted more company than our own.'[3]

The 'Birmingham Colony' included Charles Faulkner, a mathematician who became a civil engineer and a founder-member of Morris's Firm, R. W. Dixon, poet, and later Canon of Carlisle, William Fulford, 'devoured with admiration for Tennyson', who for a time was the leader of the group, and Cormell Price—'Crom'—a close friend of Morris for many years. At first Morris and Burne-Jones, both destined for the church, spent their evenings reading ecclesiastical history, but then, inspired by their friends, they turned to headier literature—their poets were Tennyson, Keats and Shelley; their novelists Thackeray, Kingsley and Dickens, and their prophets Carlyle and Ruskin. It was during Morris's first year at Oxford that the second volume of *The Stones of Venice* was published; Morris was familiar with *Modern*

Painters and the impact on him of *The Nature of Gothic* has already been described. Mackail, Morris's biographer, records a contemporary account by Dixon:

'At this time Morris was an aristocrat, and a High Churchman. His manners and tastes and sympathies were all aristocratic. His countenance was beautiful in features and expression, particularly in the expression of purity . . . It was when the Exeter men, Burne-Jones and he, got at Ruskin, that strong direction was given to a true vocation—*The Seven Lamps, Modern Painters*, and *The Stones of Venice*. It was some little time before I and the others could enter into this, but we soon saw the greatness and importance of it.'

Ruskin, a passion for poetry, paintings, old books, old churches and noble sentiments, formed the romantic backcloth to their lives—passions which were intensified by their visits to English country churches and pilgrimages to the mediaeval cities of France and Belgium. They were always aware, however, of the contrasts between past splendours and present barbarity. The Birmingham set had, of course, first-hand knowledge of what life was like in an industrial city. The 'special enthusiasms' of Price and Faulkner, according to Mackail, were 'for sanitation, for Factory Acts, for the bare elements of a possible life among the mass of their fellow citizens'. Morris, however, in these early years, opted for personal, rather than political action: 'I can't enter into politico-social subjects with any interest', he wrote at the age of twenty-three, when he was first working for Street in Oxford, 'for on the whole I see things are in a muddle, and I have no power or vocation to set them right in ever so little a degree. My work is the embodiment of dreams in one form or another . . .'[4] One of the first dreams of the set had been the establishment of a monastic order to conduct, as Burne-Jones put it 'a Crusade and Holy warfare against this age'; by 1855, when most of them were in their final year at Oxford, the Order had become a secular brotherhood of friends devoted to literary and artistic pursuits, and its mouthpiece the *Oxford and Cambridge Magazine*.

There are, of course, certain resemblances between this venture and the Pre-Raphaelite Brotherhood which had been founded seven years earlier. By this time both Morris and Burne-Jones were aware of the movement, and of its aims, as defined by Ruskin: 'Pre-Raphaelitism has but one principle, that of absolute, un-compromising truth in all that it does, obtained by working everything, down to the most minute detail, from nature only.'[5] They now became as enthusiastic about the aims of art, as revealed by Ruskin and Pre-Raphaelite paintings, as they were about literature and architecture, and the idea of a magazine to serve as a mouthpiece for their views was no doubt inspired by the Pre-Raphaelite *Germ*. The magazine, financed by Morris, ran for twelve monthly issues; it contained prose and poetry, including Morris's first published work, and some weighty articles by Faulkner on social issues (Burne-Jones produced a skittish drawing *Faulkner's Improved Sewerage* to enliven an article on sanitation, but because of the expense it could not be used). Ruskin promised to write and Rossetti sent in two poems, as well as a revised version of *The Blessed Damozel*, which had first appeared in the *Germ*.

After the revelations of Oxford neither Burne-Jones nor Morris could contemplate taking Holy Orders—Burne-Jones, by now under the spell of Rossetti, decided to become a painter, and Morris, to the consternation of his family, chose architecture. Looking like 'a wonderful bird just out of his shell'[6] he articled himself to G. E. Street, who was then architect to the diocese of Oxford, met Philip Webb who was to be a lifelong friend, and after nine months spent, according to Webb, copying a drawing of the doorway in St Augustine's Church, Canterbury ('the compass points nearly bored a hole through the drawing board'),[7] decided to attempt to become a painter. He had, while he was with Street, experimented with stone and wood carving, moulding clay and illuminating, but for the time being, inspired, like Burne-Jones, by Rossetti, he was convinced that he had found his true vocation. He left Street, who had by now moved his practice to London, and took over, with Burne-Jones, the premises in Red Lion Square that Rossetti had vacated.

Morris and Burne-Jones spent over two years in Red Lion Square and this period determined the pattern of their lives. Through Rossetti they had got to know Ruskin, who used to call on them on Thursday evenings when he had his class at the Working Men's College ('isn't it like a dream', wrote Burne-Jones);[8] Morris had some furniture made for himself—the great settle which is now at the Red House, two solid chairs 'such as Barbarossa might have sat in', and a table 'as firm, and as heavy, as a rock'. Both Burne-Jones and Morris joined Rossetti in his scheme to paint frescoes —themes from Malory on the damp plaster in the hall of the Oxford Union and both got engaged—Burne-Jones to Georgiana Macdonald, and Morris to Jane Burden.

The Pre-Raphaelites and design

By 1860 Morris, Burne-Jones and Rossetti were all married; Morris moved into the Red House that summer, but his colleagues were also furnishing and decorating their new apartments at the same time. Rossetti, for example, was designing a wallpaper for his drawing-room, planning to have it printed on 'common brown packing paper and on blue grocer's paper, to try which is best'. The paper was to be patterned with trees standing 'the whole height of the room' and the effect was to be 'sombre, but I think rich also. When we get this paper up, we shall have the doors and wainscotting painted summerhouse green'.[9]

This preoccupation with furniture and decoration, which led to the Red House collaboration and the formation of the Firm, was a reflection of a concern for the decorative arts that had preoccupied the Pre-Raphaelites and their associates for a number of years—a concern that stemmed from the general interest in design reform, as much as from their own involvement in the redefinition of art. The idea that artists should involve themselves with the so-called 'lesser arts' was after all not a new one; in the nineteenth century the principle was 'rediscovered', not only by those hoping to improve the standard of manufactured goods but by the various groups who, for one reason or another, wished to attack academic exclusiveness. The establishment of the Schools of Design was part of a campaign against the Royal

Academy, and the Pre-Raphaelites had their own war to wage against that institution. And although Madox Brown was the only member of the group associated with Pre-Raphaelitism who could be defined as a 'designer' in any contemporary sense, several of them acknowledged, with Holman Hunt, 'decorative design as part of a true artist's ambition'.

Hunt, in his autobiography *Pre-Raphaelitism and the Pre-Raphaelite Brotherhood*,[10] claimed an interest in applied design since his early years when his father was in charge of a cotton warehouse, and he himself had worked in Richard Cobden's London office, watching the 'designer' preparing patterns. By 1860 when he was sufficiently established to 'attend breakfast' with the Gladstones at Carlton House Terrace, he was prepared to give his hosts lessons in taste, criticizing their Dresden china for its 'elaborate determination to defy the fundamental principles of sound design' and 'the fitness of things'—he was, in fact, objecting to the elaborate landscapes, 'statues, cavaliers and dames dancing about' that decorated the surface. Hunt also insisted that he was the first to interest Rossetti in the wider implications of their ideals, although in this case he may well have been wise after the event.

'My past experience in pattern design and my criticisms upon the base and vulgar forms and incoherent forms in contemporary furniture, to which I drew Rossetti's attention on his first visit to me, encouraged reform in these particulars, and we speculated an improvement in all household objects, furniture, fabrics and other interior decorations . . .'

In spite of these convictions, however, which all the Pre-Raphaelites professed to share, Ford Madox Brown was not allowed to display his furniture in the exhibition of the recently formed Hogarth Club in 1859—at this stage the tolerance of 'applied art' did not stretch so far. Ford Madox Brown, a founder member of the Morris Firm, was the most consistent designer associated with the Pre-Raphaelite group, and his furniture came nearer to the ideal of robust crude simplicity, as defined in *The Nature of Gothic*, than much of the elaborate work that was to be produced by the Firm. According to Ford M. Hueffer, Madox Brown 'had designed his own furniture long before the firm of Morris & Co. was thought of',[11] and he also had experience as a teacher, both of painting and design. In 1850, for example, he became headmaster of the North London School of Design, an enterprise launched by Thomas Seddon, the painter, whose family were well-known cabinet-makers. (Seddon's venture was an early attempt to counter the government system of training; he canvassed workshops in the North London area, gathering together workmen who were only free for instruction in the evenings.) In 1858 Brown took over Rossetti's class at the Working Men's College, where, according to a pupil 'his teaching was as systematic and precise as Rossetti's had been free',[12] and he also taught at Major Gillum's Boys' Home in the Euston Road. Philip Webb was also associated with this enterprise; in 1862 he designed a row of shops for Major Gillum near Finsbury Square, and the boys made some furniture there for him to give to the Burne-Joneses as a wedding present.[13] The boys also worked for the Firm soon after it was founded, when workshops, office and showrooms were rented in Red Lion Square.

Although it remained in production until the twentieth century, not much of Madox Brown's furniture has survived; that which does, however, including a bedroom suite discovered during the restoration of Kelmscott by the Society of Antiquaries (see pl 17) is remarkably unpretentious and straightforward. This was 'artisan's' furniture, undecorated and solid, and its quality was recognized later by the Arts and Crafts generation—not only by Hueffer, who described the furniture's 'adaptation to need, solidity, a kind of homely beauty, and above all absolute dissociation from all false display, veneering and the like', in the Arts and Crafts Exhibition Society catalogue of 1896, but by the architect John Sedding, who was to question the ambivalence of his contemporaries towards machine production. Sedding saw the workman's chest of drawers on display at an earlier exhibition of the Society, and was impressed. It was, he wrote

'. . . quite a plain thing, with only a jolly, depressed carved shell above the glass and chamfered to the edges of the drawers—made in deal and stained green—that is all! It was just a commonplace thing handled imaginatively, and it gave me as much pleasure as anything in the exhibition. It made me feel that it takes a big man to do a simple thing'.[14]

There are echoes here of Philip Webb's 'I never begin to be satisfied until my work looks commonplace'—an ideal that belongs to the 1890s rather than the 1860s.

Madox Brown was undoubtedly a formidable influence on his own and the Arts and Crafts generation. In spite of the social concerns of the Birmingham set, he was the most radical of the founder members of the Firm (Morris's own commitment, of course, came later)—opening a soup kitchen for his starving neighbours in the winter of 1859–60, and later while he was in Manchester in the 1880s attempting to organize a 'labour bureau' for unemployed workmen.[15] Mackmurdo, in his unpublished *History of the Arts and Crafts Movement*, considers that he acted as a stabilizing influence on the Firm; he was, as Mackmurdo pointed out, more mature, and 'largest in experience', and, he continues 'certain it is that the group would not have been artistically and practically robust without his experience and power'.[16]

The formation of the Firm

It is not clear who actually supplied the impetus for the formation of the Firm; the idea of this kind of group enterprise was one that most of the Pre-Raphaelites had, at one time or another, entertained, and Morris stated, when he sent a prospectus to his former tutor, the Rev F. B. Guy, that this was one of the main reasons for building the Red House. Obviously the idea of an artists' collaborative crystallized when the group was working together to furnish the house and they realized that they could exercise their joint skills over a wider field. Rossetti, according to Theodore Watts-Dunton, recalled the specific occasion:

'One evening, a lot of us were together and we got talking about the way in which artists did all kinds of things in olden times, designed every kind of decoration, and most kinds of furniture, and someone suggested—as a joke more than anything else— that we could each put down five pounds and form a company. We had no idea whatever of commercial success, but it succeeded almost in our own despite.'[17]

According to William Rossetti, however, the suggestion came from Peter Paul Marshall, the engineer friend of Madox Brown,[18] which may well explain the inclusion of this 'outsider' among the founder members of the Firm, which included, as well as Morris and Marshall, the painters Rossetti, Burne-Jones and Madox Brown, the architect Philip Webb, and the mathematician Charles Faulkner from the Birmingham set.

There was, of course, some truth in the prospectus' bold contention that 'attempts of this kind hitherto have been crude and fragmentary', for although the idea that 'Artists of Reputation' should become involved with the 'Decorative Arts' had been anticipated some twenty years earlier by Henry Cole and his Summerly's Art Manufactures, there was no similar collaborative venture in existence at that time. Nevertheless the design profession was becoming reasonably well established, with Alfred Stevens, Christopher Dresser, Owen Jones and Bruce Talbert laying the foundations for their reputation in the '70s and '80s, while many of the architects associated with the Gothic Revival worked as designers (William Burges is an obvious example) or employed assistants as had Pugin in the '30s and '40s. The motivation of Morris and his colleagues, however, was very different from that of their contemporaries and predecessors. Unlike Cole they were in no way concerned to reconcile art and industry; they had absorbed Ruskin and they had no wish to compromise with commercialism. 'Art' to them meant individuality and the search for 'truth', whether in painting, architecture or applied design—and truth, they felt, could be found both in the study of nature, and in the recreation of the spirit rather than the letter of mediaevalism. Direct imitation of the Gothic was meaningless—'unfair' as Morris put it 'to the old and stupid for the present'.[19] The wider aims and the justification for the project in these early years, therefore, centred round the conviction, which was to take on more significance when Morris began to 'intellectualize' his attitudes in the '70s, that the artist should be involved with more than 'pictorial labour'[20] and that his concern was with the total environment.

Obviously, on a personal level, such an idea would appeal to Morris, who felt himself to be an artist, but who had as much difficulty with paint and canvas as he had with set-square and drawing board. But individual frustrations apart, what he and his colleagues were attempting to express was the idea of the unity of the arts that had been latent in Pre-Raphaelite theory. To the 'painterly' vision of the Pre-Raphaelites, however, there was added the ideal of the vernacular, as expressed by Philip Webb, who saw architecture as 'a common tradition of honest building' and who had built the Red House, with its great oak staircase, oak beams, red-tiled hall and large brick chimney-pieces as an expression of that vision. Almost immediately, therefore, a certain duality was apparent in the work and attitudes of the Firm—a duality that was to recur in the products of the Arts and Crafts movement. On the one hand there was the straightforward, honest craftsmanship—in the Ruskinian sense—as represented by the workaday furniture of Madox Brown and Webb's glassware for James Powell (see pl 14), which in their directness and simplicity have a definite twentieth-century feeling; the stained glass, tapestries, embroideries and elaborately painted furniture on the other hand, in spite of the radicalism that inspired them, are more closely bound by mid-nineteenth-century ornamental conventions—although they reveal how idealism and conviction could transform those conventions into something unique (pls 18 and 19).

Ironically enough, however, it was for their skill as imitators, rather than innovators, that the group was first singled out for public praise. The occasion—the International Exhibition at South Kensington in 1862—marked the beginning of the Firm's commercial success (according to Mackail £150 worth of goods were sold from the stands), and the exhibits, which included stained glass, embroideries, furniture, tiles, table-glass and candlesticks, were awarded two gold medals. 'Messrs Morris & Company', stated the jury, 'have exhibited several pieces of furniture, tapestries, etc., in the style of the Middle Ages. The general forms of the furniture, the arrangement of the tapestry, and the character of the details are satisfying to the archaeologist from the exactness of the imitation, at the same time that the general effect is excellent.'[21]

As far as the stained glass was concerned, the 'exactness of imitation' was such that competitors in the trade were convinced that the company had used genuine mediaeval glass, and it was from this time that the Firm's contempt for contemporary commercial practice seems to have become apparent. Lewis Day, for example, has described how he first came to hear of the Firm's activities in 1866 and asked 'an old hand at design' who they were. The answer was: 'A set of amateurs who are going to teach us our trade'.[22] In many ways, of course, he was right.

The 'trades' that the Firm became involved in in the early years, resulted from private commissions, either for stained glass, furniture or interiors. From the beginning stained glass proved to be the most important part of their production, and since Rossetti, Burne-Jones, Madox Brown and Webb had all, to a varying extent, already worked in this medium, they were in a good position to consolidate their experience in group practice. Their most important commissions came from G. T. Bodley, and from work for him at Brighton, Scarborough and Selsley stemmed a whole series of commissions that were maintained throughout the life of the Firm. The work on stained glass was very much a corporate venture in the early years, with the partners contributing details to the design. According to Lethaby, Webb planned the layout of the early windows,[23] insisting on thick iron bars between the panels ('My dear fellow, they improve it'); he also drew the animals, the lettering and the heraldic details. Overall responsibility, however, lay with Morris, who chose the colours and usually worked out the leading, and who passed the fired glass for inclusion in the final design. A distinctive style emerged that differentiated

Morris glass from contemporary production, not only in the sensitive and dramatic use of colour and the characteristic intensity of the figures but in the elaboration of their settings; the stylized yet naturalistic trees, foliage, flowers, and the lovingly delineated fabrics, hangings, pottery, jugs and household impedimenta that formed part of the painting tradition were re-created in the glass, which grew more inventive as the partners gained wider experience of the possibilities of the medium. In 1883 when the glass was exhibited at the Boston Foreign Fair, a handout was produced describing how the work was conditioned by the potential and limitations of the medium:

'As regards the method of painting and the design, our glass differs so much from other kinds that we may be allowed a word of apology. Glass painting differs from oil and fresco, mostly in the translucency of the material and the strength, amounting to absolute blackness of the outlines. The blackness of outline is due to the use of lead frames or settings, which are absolutely necessary for the support of the pieces of glass if various colours are used. It is therefore a condition and characteristic of glass painting. Absolute blackness of outline and translucency of colour are then the differentia between glass painting and panel or wall painting. They lead to treatment, quite peculiar in its principles of light and shade and composition. In the first place the drawing and composition have to be much more simple, and yet more carefully studied, than in paintings which have all the assistance of shadows and reflected lights to disguise faults and assist the grouping. In the next place the light and shade must be so managed that the strong outlines shall not appear crude, nor the work within it thin; this implies a certain conventionalism of treatment, and makes the details of a figure so much more an affair of drawing than of painting; because by drawing—that is, by filling the outlines with other lines of proportionate strength— the force of the predominant lines is less unnatural. These, then, are the first conditions of good glass painting as we perceive them—well-balanced and shapely figures, pure and simple drawing, and a minimum of light and shade. There is another reason for this last. Shading is a dulling of the glass; it is therefore inconsistent with the use of a material which was chosen for its brightness. After these we ask for beautiful colour. There may be more of it, or less; but it is only rational and becoming that the light we stain should not be changed to dirt or ugliness. Colour, pure and sweet, is the least you should ask for in a painted window.'[24]

Definitions of the design process

Volume upon volume, in the nineteenth century, was devoted to the theory and practice of design, but Morris's contribution is outstanding, not only because he was a poet and knew how to manipulate words but because he was a practitioner and all his theories carry the conviction of personal involvement in the processes he is describing. He rarely provided his followers with neat definitions of 'good design', but he did on various occasions enumerate the principles upon which he based his practice, and it was from these essays and lectures, which began to appear in the late 1870s, that the Arts and Crafts philosophy of design was to evolve.

The cardinal principle upon which all his theory rested centred round his conviction that the designer (or architect) must have a personal knowledge of the potentials and limitations of the materials he is working with if he is to produce work of any validity, and such understanding of the processes of design must be learned at first hand; it cannot be communicated by a teacher, or a book.

'Never forget the material you are working with, and try always to use it for doing what it can do best: if you feel yourself hampered by the material in which you are working, instead of being helped by it, you have so far not learned your business, any more than a would-be poet has, who complains of the hardship of writing in measure and rhyme. The special limitations of the material should be a pleasure to you, not a hindrance: a designer, therefore, should always thoroughly understand the process of the special manufacture he is dealing with, or the result will be a mere *tour de force*. On the other hand, it is the pleasure of understanding the capabilities of the special material, and using them for suggesting (not imitating) natural beauty and incident, that gives the *raison d'être* for decorative art.'

Morris was talking about textiles,[25] but the passage can be taken to refer to the whole design process; it sums up the philosophy of Morris's working life—a philosophy which had evolved as Morris became more totally absorbed by the work of the Firm.

Following the success of the 1862 exhibition, and the commissions for stained glass, it was apparent that the Firm might, if its activities were properly organized and channelled, become financially viable. By 1865 Morris was becoming increasingly responsible for the day-to-day running of the Firm, and in that year he decided, reluctantly, to abandon the Red House in order to concentrate the Firm's activities in London. He took over premises in Queen's Square, Bloomsbury, and appointed Warington Taylor, described by Madox Brown as a 'man of business-like habits',[26] to replace Charles Faulkner, who had gone back to Oxford, as business manager of the Firm. The next year the Firm gained two valuable commissions—to decorate the Armoury and Tapestry Room at St James's Palace, and the Green Dining Room at South Kensington; this seal of official approval, together with Warington Taylor's unorthodox but sound endeavours to keep the group to their deadlines and to persuade them not to undercharge, helped to put the Firm on a sounder financial footing.

The move to Queen's Square also coincided with Morris's first attempts to design wallpapers—an indication of his growing preoccupation with pattern design. The Firm was already producing embroideries and painted tiles for private commissions (see pl 16) and in 1864 Morris had designed three papers, *Daisy*, *Trellis* and *Fruit*, using motifs from nature—flowers, fruit and birds (drawn by Webb)—in somewhat rigidly formalized repeats. No doubt to his contemporaries, whether educated to the elaborate conventionalized abstractions favoured by South Kensington, or seduced by the lush *trompe l'œil* foliage that the reformers despised, these patterns seemed somewhat unsophisticated. In any event their sales were not encouraging and no more were designed until 1871. From then on, however, his range increased, and he continued to produce wallpapers until the 1890s, all hand-printed from wood-blocks by Jeffrey & Co. There were few problems here, but his struggles to achieve the colours, rhythms and textures he required in fabrics and carpets have become part of the Morris legend. He had designed his first chintz *Tulip and Willow* in 1873, and because of his dissatisfaction with the printing, he began experimenting with dyes at Queen's Square in 1874. George Wardle was now manager of the Firm,* and his brother Thomas had a dye-works in Leek in Staffordshire; during the next two years Morris paid frequent visits to Leek and determined to abandon textile design if he could not achieve the high standards he required. This involved a complete boycott of all commercial dyes and a reinvestigation of those methods 'which are at least as old as Pliny, who speaks of them as being old in his time'.[27]

Morris was able to start his own dyeing at Queen's Square, and this continued on a more ambitious scale following his move to Merton Abbey, in Surrey, in 1881. Here the River Wandle supplied water which was ideal for dyeing, and the Firm began to print its own chintzes. 'We had a dye house appropriate to them', wrote George Wardle, 'and other necessary "ageing" rooms, etc., etc; we had also a dye house for silk and wool and blue vats for silk, wool and cotton. There was an abundance of pure water, light and air.'[28]

During the decade following the move to Merton Morris extended his range of carpets, as well as producing more tapestries and hand-tufted rugs. He also produced a magnificent series of fabrics, including *Brother Rabbit*, *Strawberry Thief*, *Eyebright*, *Cray*, *Evenlode* and *Wandle*:

'Their beautifully controlled colours, the combination of delicacy and boldness in the drawing of the flowers, and the rich and masterly elaboration of their patterning seemed like a breath of fresh air to a generation tired of the stale clichés of the ordinary furnishings, so that already by the early 1880s "Morris chintzes" were a household word in both England and the United States. Indeed, so great was their reputation that many late Victorian families made it a point of honour to have nothing but Morris papers and fabrics in their houses.'[29]

The commentator here is Peter Floud, who through his researches at the Victoria and Albert Museum, London, and by means of the exhibition 'Victorian and Edwardian Decorative Arts' organized by the Museum in 1952, demonstrated for the first time Morris's relationships to his contemporary designers. For, as we have seen, Morris was not alone in attempting to improve standards in pattern design; he had predecessors in Pugin, Owen Jones and Redgrave (see pls 1 and 64) and an exact contemporary in Christopher Dresser, and his endeavours must be seen against the background of their attempts to educate the designer and his client. From them Morris had absorbed certain conventions: he insisted, as was logical, on 'geometrical structure' in recurring patterns, and said that pattern on carpets 'should lie absolutely flat upon the ground';[30] like Redgrave and Jones he suggests appropriate colours

* Warington Taylor had died in 1870, and George Wardle, who had been associated with the Firm since the early '60s, acting as draughtsman and book-keeper, took his place.

to use: 'in designing carpets the method of *contrast* is the best one to employ, and blue and red, quite frankly used, with white or very light outlines on a dark ground, and black or some very dark colours on a light background, are the main colours on which the designer should depend'. His insistence on 'truth to nature' was, of course, no innovation, and at this time the theory was being re-emphasized by Christopher Dresser, who had studied botany and had joined the staff of the Schools of Design in 1859, and who saw 'in vegetable nature the utmost regard to fitness' as well as 'structure, force, energy and the inherent order of growth.'[31]

Here, however, the resemblance ends, for Morris was a far better pattern designer and a far more persuasive theorist than any of his contemporaries, and as Lethaby was to point out 'his work will necessarily remain supreme until as great a man as Morris again deals with that manner of expression with his *full force* as he did'.[32] The imagery he uses when he designs his fabrics and when he writes about them carries the conviction of genius, for here is nature seen through the eyes of an artist translated into designs that had and still have no equal, and which were backed up by a theory expressed with forceful and vigorous clarity. He had no time for the 'meaningless stripes and spots and other tormentings of the simple twill of the web, which are so common in the woven ornament of the eighteenth century and in our own times'.[33] As a 'Western man and a picture lover' he insisted on 'plenty of meaning in your patterns; I must have unmistakeable suggestions of gardens and fields, and strange trees, boughs and tendrils, or I can't do with your patterns'. According to Morris, patterns should express the vigour and growth of the plant form that inspired them: 'even where a line ends it should look as if it had plenty of capacity for more growth if it so would'. But above all, pattern, in whatever medium, should have the inevitability of nature: 'Do not introduce any lines or objects which cannot be explained by the structure of the pattern; it is just this logical sequence of form, this growth which looks as if, under the circumstances, it could not have been otherwise, which prevents the eye wearying of the repetition of the pattern.'[34] Nevertheless, Morris would never have advocated a completely spontaneous approach; a study of past achievements was essential: 'you must study the history of your art', he told his audiences, 'or you will be nose led by the first bad copyist of it that you come across'. From then on, however, the design process, based on an understanding both of the past, and of the potential of the materials used, was an entirely personal one.

Because he valued the personal above the impersonal, Morris condemned the 'mechanical' in all aspects of design, and categorized the design processes according to the amount of freedom they gave him as an artist and a 'picture lover'. In his essay on 'Textiles', for example, he declared that tapestry 'in which there is nothing mechanical' was the 'noblest of the weaving arts', and he distinguished between 'genuine or hand-made carpets' and 'the mechanically made carpets of today which must be looked upon as makeshifts for cheapness sake'. Similarly, when he was lecturing to potters in Burslem in 1881 he told them that if they had to 'design for machine work, at least let your design show clearly what it is. Make it mechanical with a vengeance, at the same time as simple as possible. Don't try, for instance, to make a printed plate look like a hand-painted one.' He looked either for total richness, or total simplicity in design—these, for him, were two sides of the same coin.

Furniture, he believed, also fell into two distinct categories. On the one hand there was the 'necessary workaday furniture', which should be kept 'simple to the last degree' and on the other what he called 'state-furniture': 'we need not spare ornament on these, but make them as elegant and elaborate as we can with carving or inlaying or painting; these are the blossoms of the art of furniture'.[35] This, of course, describes the practice of the Firm, which in the early years had produced variants of the Sussex rush-seated chair (pls 22, 23), Madox Brown's artisan's furniture, and more ambitious cabinets, chests and wardrobes with painted panels. And in spite of Warington Taylor's plea for the production of 'moveable furniture, light, Sir—something you can pull about with one hand'[36] it was on the 'prestige' pieces that the efforts of the Firm were concentrated. Perhaps it was because Morris himself was not directly involved in the design and production of furniture that the Firm's achievements in this field were not sustained. When George Jack, Mervyn Macartney and W. A. S. Benson were involved in the cabinet-making of the 1880s, several elaborate designs were produced, embellished with marquetry and inlays, and where Benson was involved, silver mounts and hinges (see pl 21), but these pieces have less charm and conviction than contemporary designs by Voysey, Gimson and Ambrose Heal. Yet the impetus for the achievements of these craftsmen had stemmed from the work of Madox Brown and Webb, and from Morris's own design philosophy, as expressed in his lectures and writing after 1877.

The democracy of art

When Morris gave his first public lecture on *The Decorative Arts* to the Trades Guild of Learning in 1877, he was well known both as a decorator and poet. The Firm had opened new showrooms in Oxford Street some months earlier, and he had been in complete control of the business since 1875 when the original partnership was dissolved. By this time, however, he was becoming increasingly concerned with social and political problems; in 1876 he had joined the ranks of Liberal dissenters against Disraeli's support of Turkey in the Russo-Turkish controversy, and in 1877, as secretary to the Eastern Question Association he had written a pamphlet *Unjust War* which took the form of a manifesto 'to the working men of England'. At the same time he had initiated the formation of 'Anti-Scrape'—the Society for the Protection of Ancient Buildings, and to Morris these seemingly disparate causes had a common root—for he judged both issues in terms of a class struggle. On the one hand there were the 'greedy gamblers on the Stock Exchange', the 'idle officers' and the 'Tory Rump' taking every opportunity to bind the working man 'hand and foot forever to irresponsible capital', and on the other there were the 'modern architect, parson and squire', themselves bound by 'interest, habit and ignorance' and bent on the destruction of the 'sacred monuments of the nation's growth and hope'. The target in both cases was the working man—the past he had created with his own hands was threatened and his future was jeopardized because society put a higher value on the counting house than on the workshop.

It was with these convictions that Morris embarked on his lectures, which defined his campaign for the democracy of art as part of a wider campaign for social justice. 'I do not want art for a few, any more than education for a few, or freedom for a few', he had declared in his first lecture in 1877, and by 1880 he is describing his mission in terms of a cause and a crusade:

'. . . surely since we are servants of a Cause, hope must be ever with us, and sometimes perhaps it will so quicken our vision that it will outrun the slow lapse of time, and show us the victorious days when millions of those who now sit in darkness will be enlightened by an *Art made by the people and for the people, a joy to the maker and the user*.'[37]

From such a generous and spontaneous collaboration a 'decorative, noble, popular art' would emerge, simple, organic and close to the earth, with a natural unity between form, function and decoration: 'For . . . everything made by man's hand has a form, which must be either beautiful or ugly; beautiful if it is in accord with nature, and helps her; ugly if it is discordant with nature, and thwarts her.' These man-made 'forms and intricacies' need not necessarily imitate nature, but the craftsman must work as nature does 'till the web, the cup or the knife, look as natural, nay as lovely, as the green field, the river bank, or the mountain flint'.[38] These aims, however, could never be achieved until the complex structure of contemporary life was simplified for: 'Simplicity of life, begetting simplicity of taste, that is a love for sweet and lofty things, is of all matters most necessary for the birth of the new and better art we crave for; simplicity everywhere, in the palace as well as in the cottage.'[39]

Morris here is reiterating the values he had absorbed from Ruskin, values that had been reinforced by some fifteen years' practical experience as a craftsman. He was, of course, aware that in the type of commission he was undertaking he was 'ministering to the swinish luxury of the rich'.[40] The fact that his own designs were beyond the means of the majority angered and frustrated him; but he wanted no less than perfection, and perfection, as he conceived it, could not be achieved through compromise with a system, which, he believed was dedicated to the destruction of freedom, individuality and beauty. The fact that goods designed according to his standards were expensive was in itself an indictment of the situation in which he found himself, and it was the clash between his personal ideals of craftsmanship, and the reality of commercial practice, that led him to political commitment. His Socialism, which was, as he explained in his letter to Andreas Scheu, an Austrian refugee and fellow socialist, 'Socialism seen through the eyes of an artist', was the inevitable outcome of his work as a designer: 'Both my historical studies and my practical conflict with the philistinism of modern society have *forced* on me the conviction that art cannot have a real life and growth under the present system of commercialism and profit-mongering.'[41]

Morris formally allied himself to Socialism in 1883 when he joined the Democratic Federation (later to become the Social Democratic Federation). He joined because he felt bound 'to act for the destruction of the system which seems to me mere oppression and obstruction',[42] and his ultimate aim was 'to obtain for the whole people, duly organised, the possession and control of all the means of production and exchange, destroying at the same time all national rivalries'.[43] Fundamental to this aim, however, was his belief in the necessity of art as a redemptive force in society, since 'you cannot educate, you cannot civilise men, unless you can give them a share in art',[44] and art is 'as necessary to man as his daily bread'.

The conviction that a Socialist democracy would ensure collaboration rather than competition, and that this collaboration would lead ultimately to the situation in which 'the glorious art of architecture, now for some time slain by commercial greed, would be born again and flourish',[45] led several designers and architects in the 1880s and '90s to embrace the Socialist cause. Of the founder members of the Firm both Webb and Faulkner gave Morris their full support; Walter Crane, the first president of the Arts and Crafts Exhibition Society joined the Socialist League in 1884; both Ashbee and Mackmurdo were involved in plans for socialistic reconstruction, and Norman Shaw's office, while Lethaby was there, gained such a reputation that fathers were loath to allow their sons to associate with the staff.

Morris remained a socialist to the end of his life, although his relationships with the 'professionals' were never easy, and he was forced to resign, first from the SDF, and then, a more bitter blow, from the Socialist League, which he had helped to found, and whose journal *The Commonweal* he had edited. But although he could write to Georgiana Burne-Jones 'I half wish that I had not been born with a sense of romance and beauty in this accursed age'[46] he remained convinced that 'the defence of order and a decent life'[47] were fundamental to the socialist cause. The weapons with which to fight this battle were education—not mere book-learning, but education of the whole man, and the proper use of the nation's resources, both natural and technical. For Morris, once committed to the ideal of a socialist state, was forced to revise and re-think his attitudes to machine production. As a craftsman and an individualist, he loathed the impersonality of the machine, which chained men to its service and made slaves of them; in his role as a craftsman he saw the machine at best as a tool, an extension of the hand, to be used for processes which the designer could control. As a humanitarian he saw concrete evidence of the miseries that the Industrial Revolution had created, but at the same time he realized that society could not function without mechanization, and he came to recognize that the machine, properly used, might become a force for liberation. He might have told the potters of Burslem 'set yourself as much as possible against all machine work (this to all men)',[48] but this was in 1881. During the 1880s his attitude began to change, and in 1884 he was claiming that 'those almost miraculous machines, which if orderly forethought had dealt with them, might even now be speedily extinguishing all irksome and unintelligent labour, leaving us free to raise the standard of skill of hand and energy of mind in our workmen'.[49]

H

He realized that his *volte-face* might seem a betrayal, and might antagonize some of his colleagues, for to 'people of the artistic turn of mind, machinery is particularly distasteful, and they will be apt to say you will never get your surroundings pleasant so long as you are surrounded by machinery. I don't quite admit that; it is the allowing of machines to be our masters, and not our servants, that so injures the beauty of life nowadays.'[50] The factory, in fact, was to become an essential part of the community in Morris's vision of the socialist future; it would be set in pleasant surroundings and its buildings would be well designed, for 'there would be no serious difficulty in making them beautiful, as every building might be which serves its purpose duly, which is built generously as regards material, and which is built with pleasure by the builders and designers'.[51] There would be a dining hall, study areas and a school within each complex, and the factory would 'make no sordid litter, befoul no water, nor poison the air with smoke'. It would produce 'goods useful to the community' and 'provide for its own workers work light in duration'; it would be a true 'palace of industry' adorned with painting and sculpture, and its output would be worth having, since it would be controlled by workers who 'will know well what good work and true finish (not trade finish) means', and who would be catering for a discriminating public.[52]

The vision of the machine so perfected and controlled that it would leave us free to get on with the real business of living, is a potent one; it recurs throughout the nineteenth century and it remains the ideal for an automated society. Fundamental to Morris's Utopia, however, was the conviction that man, so liberated, would learn to love and create art: 'People living under the conditions of life above mentioned,' wrote Morris in *A Factory as it Might be*, 'having manual skill, technical and general education, and leisure to use these advantages, are quite sure to develop a love of art, that is to say, a sense of beauty and interest in life, which in the long run must stimulate them to the desire for artistic creation, the satisfaction of which is of all pleasures the greatest'.[53] Materialism and mass consumption may have created other goals, but before dismissing Morris's Utopia, it is perhaps worth recording the comments of his contemporary, Oscar Wilde: 'A map of the world that does not include Utopia', he wrote, 'is not worth even glancing at, for it leaves out the one country at which humanity is always landing. And when humanity lands there, it looks out, and seeing a better country, it sets sail. Progress is the realization of Utopias.'[54]

The Kelmscott Press

The Kelmscott Press was Morris's swan song; he founded it in 1890, the year which marked his break with the Socialist League, and when he died six years later he had issued over fifty titles, including the *Chaucer*, the *Nature of Gothic* and his own *Earthly Paradise*. The Press was founded on the principles, fundamental to the Arts and Crafts movement, that 'a work of utility might also be a work of art, if we cared to make it so',[55] and it gave a further impetus to a preoccupation with fine printing that had been maintained throughout the century, in spite of the overall lowering of standards that the introduction of machine techniques in printing and the growth of a mass market had entailed. For in establishing the Kelmscott Press, and above all in defining his aims for it, Morris, as with so many of his enterprises, gave a new impetus and new interpretation to ideas that were already latent, and he also laid the foundations for the twentieth-century renaissance in typography and book design.

A book, according to Morris, should be conceived as architecture, each detail contributing to the whole, so that the paper, the ink, the type-faces, the word and line spacing, the placing of the margins and the integration of illustration and decoration all had to be considered in detail, and in relation to the complete book. These ideas, as Morris pointed out, had already been put forward by Emery Walker and were published in the Arts and Crafts Exhibition Society's first catalogue in 1888; the Kelmscott Press was Morris's interpretation of Walker's philosophy and a demonstration of how books, as he conceived them, ought to look. His paper was handmade to his own specifications by a firm in Kent and a limited number of copies were printed on vellum; his ink came from Hanover, and because he had no time for available type-faces he designed his own—the *Golden* type based on a fifteenth-century face by Jenson, and *Troy* and *Chaucer* designed to 'redeem the Gothic character from the charge of unreadableness that is commonly brought against it'.[56] Burne-Jones drew most of the illustrations, which were printed from wood-blocks, although some illustrations were provided by Walter Crane (see pl 33) and Arthur Gaskin; Morris himself designed most of the title pages and more than 600 borders and initials—Lethaby who watched him at work, has described how the 'forms were led along and bent over and rounded at the edges with definite pleasure, they were *stroked* into place as it were with a sensation like that of smoothing a cat . . . It was to express this sensuous pleasure that he used to say that all good designing work was felt in the stomach.'[57]

This sensuous pleasure in the look and the feel of a book, together with the intellectual conception of how its basic elements should be structured and controlled, combined to revolutionize book production and typography in both Europe and the United States. During the 1890s several private presses were established in England, including Ashbee's Essex House Press, the Ashendene Press founded by St John Hornby in 1894, Rickett's Vale Press, Pissarro's Eragny Press and the Doves Press, founded by T. J. Cobden-Sanderson and Emery Walker in 1900. All were directly inspired by Morris; Pissarro, for example, despairing of achieving the standards he required in France, has described how he came to London when 'William Morris's "Arts and Crafts" movement was in full swing'.[58] Ashbee took over Kelmscott equipment as well as several of Morris's craftsmen, and T. J. Cobden-Sanderson founded the Doves Press in order to express his own brand of Arts and Crafts mysticism which linked 'the wholeness, symmetry, harmony, beauty without stress or strain, of the Book Beautiful' with 'that WHOLE OF LIFE WHICH IS CONSTITUTED OF OURSELVES AND THE WORLD'.[59]

In each case, however, it was Morris's theory, rather than his practice, that provided the impetus, for the achievements of each press were varied and individualistic. The theory inspired the Art Nouveau book and the decorative experiments of the 1890s, just as it inspired the individualism and the variety of Art Nouveau product design. But at the same time Morris, through his painstaking studies of calligraphy, letter-forms and Italian Renaissance printing, had laid down the fundamental principles of good typography. His conviction that books could be 'beautiful by force of mere typography', as reflected in the achievements of the Ashendene and Doves Presses, inspired a vigorous re-appraisal of type design. The pioneers of the typographic revolution—Van de Velde in Belgium, Kalf, Enschedé, de Roos, Van Royen and Van Krimpen in the Netherlands, Koch in Germany and Rogers and Updike in the United States, all acknowledged their debt to Morris, and through them the craft ideals began to influence commercial practice. 'Our stock-in-trade', wrote Francis Meynell of the Nonesuch Press, 'has been the theory that mechanical means could be made to serve fine ends; that the machine in printing was a controllable tool.'[60] And as recently as 1958 Carl Rollins, printer to the Yale University Press, wrote: 'I am sure that I was influenced by Morris to a greater or less degree in everything that I ever did . . . it was probably because of Morris that I have become a printer.'[61]

4   Guilds and guildsmen

'I never forget when William Morris died. A handful of us were passing the *Western Daily Mercury* office, Plymouth, to attend a socialist branch meeting, and the news just choked us. A crowd of workers had assembled to see a football result. The announcement was made that "Mr William Morris died today". "Who the hell's he?" said a worker to another. Just after we heard a deafening roar. The Bashites had won!'[1] But when Morris died in October 1896 it seemed, to a handful of his colleagues at least, that a bridgehead had been secured, and that the battle against the Bashites might be won, if not in their own generation, at least in that of their successors. Within a month of Morris's death, a new art school had opened in London with William Lethaby as joint principal; the school was to be 'devoted to the teaching of art in its approach to the crafts', and most of its staff were members of the Art-Workers' Guild, that 'spiritual oasis in the wilderness of modern life' which had been founded in 1884. Two years before this Mackmurdo had established his Century Guild; C. R. Ashbee launched his Guild and School of Handicraft in London's East End in 1888, and in that same year the Arts and Crafts Exhibition Society, which aimed to be more than an oasis, had been established.

The Arts and Crafts Exhibition Society, the magazine *Studio*, which was launched in 1893 and a flourishing 'art industry' all contributed to the growing prestige of British design and design theory. During the 1890s the Arts and Crafts Exhibition Society began to exhibit regularly abroad; the first of its exhibitions was held in Brussels in 1891 where it inspired a similar organization *L'Association pour l'Art*. More significant was its impact on *Les Vingt*, a society which had been established in Belgium in 1884 to promote the work of *avant-garde* painters, and which ten years later was re-formed as *La Libre Esthétique*, dedicated to the unification of all the arts. In the following years Belgium, through the auspices of *Les Vingt* and the Arts and Crafts Exhibition Society, saw the work of Madox Brown, Morris, De Morgan, Ashbee, Sumner, Crane, Mackmurdo and Voysey, as well as that of Beardsley and the Glasgow 'outsiders'. Van de Velde, who had trained as a painter, joined *Les Vingt* and changed his vocation; before he was appointed artistic adviser on arts and industries to the Grand Duke of Saxe-Weimar in 1902 he had worked as a typographer, architect, interior designer and furniture designer, and had communicated his enthusiasm for British ideals and achievements in a series of lectures and articles. In 1896 he had been invited to design interiors for Samuel Bing's shop in Paris, *L'Art Nouveau*, and it was Bing who wrote: 'When English creations began to appear a cry of delight sounded throughout Europe. Its echo can still be heard in every country.'[2] The same year the Prussian Board of Trade, anxious to emulate British achievements, sent its emissary Hermann Muthesius on a fact-finding mission to London, and in 1898 the Grand Duke of Hesse, founding an artists' colony in Darmstadt, commissioned furniture from Ashbee and Baillie Scott.

Similar enthusiasm for art and craftsmanship were becoming evident in the United States; Louis Comfort Tiffany, who knew and admired the work of William Morris, had been working as an interior designer since 1878 calling his firm Louis C. Tiffany Company, Associated Artists. On a less exalted level there was the Roycroft phenomenon, inspired by Elbert Hubbard, an enthusiastic simple lifer with a gift for making money. In the 1880s Hubbard, who had amassed a modest fortune working as a salesman and advertising agent in Chicago, decided to travel. He came to England, met William Morris, and fired by his example, returned to found the Roycroft Institution in East Aurora, New York. This became a thriving community of pseudo-craftsmen, and in the 1920s, according to a contemporary brochure, employed 300 workmen while 'four hundred stores, scattered from Maine to California' sold 'Roycroft wrought copper and modeled leather'. There was a Roycroft Inn 'the haven of tired businessmen, the rendezvous of honeymooners, travelers and congenial souls' and a print shop and bindery 'always busy getting out Elbert Hubbard's works'.[3] These were self-consciously and crudely printed on thick, cheap paper, with clumsy Art Nouveau initials and ornaments. They were far from beautiful but they had a vast circulation and brought a somewhat eccentric version of Morris's ideals to a wide audience. (The first of Hubbard's *Little Journeys to the Homes of the Great*, a popular series, was to Kelmscott House.)

Ashbee visited the Roycrofters in the 1890s and was not impressed; Walter Crane also visited the States in 1890, and designed a mosaic for the floor of a bank in Cleveland, Ohio,[4] but one of the first ambassadors of the new ideals was Oscar Wilde, who had made his famous lecture tour in 1882, advocating 'Stately and simple architecture for your cities, bright and simple dress for your men and women' as the 'conditions of a real artistic movement'.[5] There was an obvious duality in English ideals and achievements in the 1890s, but the English designers saw no ambiguity in this appeal both to simplicity and sophistication. 'The great advantage and charm of the Morrisian method', wrote Walter Crane, 'is that it lends itself to either simplicity or splendour. You might be almost plain enough to please Thoreau, with a rush-bottomed chair, piece of matting, and oaken trestle-table; or you might have gold and lustre (the choice ware of William De Morgan) gleaming from the side-board, and jewelled light in your windows, and walls hung with rich arras tapestry.'[6]

To the Arts and Crafts generation both approaches, the simple and the luxurious, were equally valid; both sprang from the ideal of the craftsman as artist, and from the belief in individualism and individual commitment. Both reflected the designer's concern with nature and the organic rather than with accepted conventions of ornament and structure, and both, of course, contributed to the development of the movement that came to be known as 'Art Nouveau'. The English designers were to deny this changeling child of theirs; according to Walter Crane, whose work has all the hallmarks of the style, Art Nouveau was a 'strange decorative disease';[7] Voysey maintained that it was 'out of harmony with our national character and climate'[8] and the Arts and Crafts Exhibition Society never again invited the Glasgow Four to show their work after their first contribution in 1896. Nevertheless, English attitudes contributed to the development of Art Nouveau and English designers in the 1880s and '90s produced work displaying many of the characteristics of the movement. One of the first of these was Arthur Heygate Mackmurdo, whose Century Guild, founded in 1882, was to both reflect and reinterpret the craft ideal.

Mackmurdo and the Century Guild

Mackmurdo was an extraordinarily complex man whose life spans nearly a century (1851–1942). There are glimpses of the formative influences of his childhood in the various notes he left for an autobiography.[9] In one place, for example, he describes how he was not allowed to read until the age of seven and how (like Frank Lloyd Wright) he 'found delight in building structures with wooden bricks of which I had a generous collection'. He also describes how his father 'was practically interested in science, and my mother was genuinely interested in the art movement leading up to the 1851 exhibition of Mechanics, Science and Art—the absorbing interest at the period when the die of my life was being cast'. Science and Art, he adds, 'have been my absorbing interests—all Science leading up to a Social Science, all Art leading to the perfection and joy of life—individual and collective'. At the age of eighteen Mackmurdo decided to become an architect and was apprenticed to T. Chatfield Clarke in London. He was not impressed by this initiation: 'When I had completed my apprenticeship to an Architect and Surveyor in the City of London I was as ignorant of architecture as when I entered this architect's office. I knew nothing of art.' He was extending his interests in philosophy and science, however, and during this early period in London, he heard Huxley and Tindall at London University as well as attending lectures at South Kensington. He also began to read Ruskin, and already in possession of a fine presbyterian social conscience, he resolved to carry out social work in the East End of London. There he saw the churches that James Brooks was building and felt them to be the works of a genius. (Lethaby was to call them 'big-boned churches which have building power and dignity'.[10]) Although Brooks did not normally accept pupils, Mackmurdo persuaded the architect to make an exception in his case, and he was taken on as assistant. When he was working for Brooks, Mackmurdo began to experience the difficulties facing the architect who hoped to control every detail of his work. Unity of design which, as Mackmurdo was to explain, was essential if architecture were to become an 'organic' and 'vital' art, could only be achieved 'if the decorator and furnisher are craftsmen with souls awake to the inspirations and needs of their day—artists in fact'. According to Mackmurdo, Brooks designed

'every single incidental object and ornament which went into the furnishing and decoration of his building. But the execution of these designs must needs be delegated to other hands, and here was the difficulty. The repeated trials, the constant failures in getting these designs carried out with any degree of artistic sympathy, or fine sense of craftsmanship, well nigh drove the man mad.'

Mackmurdo therefore resolved, while he was working with Brooks, that he would some day make a practical attempt to remedy the situation—a resolve that was re-inforced by his further studies of Ruskin.

Mackmurdo read the instalments of *Fors Clavigera* as they appeared in 1871, and was so impressed that he began to attend Ruskin's School of Drawing at Oxford and so have access to the Master. Ruskin evidently approved of this admirer—they travel-led to Italy together in 1874, and Mackmurdo, unlike Morris, was deeply impressed by Italian Renaissance architecture. When he returned Mackmurdo taught with Ruskin at the Working Men's College. The formative influence on Mackmurdo's theory of design, therefore, was Ruskin, and it was Ruskin's teaching, as well as his experience with Brooks, which lay behind the ideals and the nomenclature of his Century Guild. Like Morris, whom he met in 1877, Mackmurdo taught himself various crafts before he launched the scheme: 'I schooled myself in the techniques of modelling and carving', he writes, 'trying my hand at some ornamental stonework for the first house I built. I learned to do repoussé work in brass . . . and embroidery. Under a skilled cabinet maker I learned enough about materials and constructive processes to design pieces of furniture.'

By 1882, when he founded the Guild, Mackmurdo had been practising as an architect for seven years, and for the past two years had been living at 20 Fitzroy Street, which, in the 1890s, became what William Rothenstein was to call the 'fashion-able unfashionable artists' quarter'. Although he insisted that he lived there in 'semi-monastic seclusion', he entertained a wide circle of friends, among them Whistler, Yeats and Ford Madox Brown, whom he greatly admired. He claimed that he 'discovered' the young Frank Brangwyn, gave him a studio in the Fitzroy Street house and introduced him to Morris; he organized a music circle to play early English music, and with his friends 'laid deep plots for Ibsen's plays upon a London stage'. Sir William Rothenstein in his *Men and Memories* describes the household in 1899 when his brother Albert came to live in London and took a room in the Mack-murdo house:

'It was an Adam house, with large lofty rooms; Selwyn Image, and his wife now had rooms there; so had Henry Carte with his son Geoffrey. They all had meals together at an ancient oak table, without a cloth, of course; in the middle stood a plaster figure and four bowls of bay which, I noticed, were covered in dust. Mackmurdo believed in the simple life. He was also very unworldly, and had let a room to my brother, and to someone else at that time. This was awkward for each of the tenants; Mackmurdo saw this too, and in the end my brother got the room to himself.'[11]

Mackmurdo, therefore, bridges the generation of the '70s and that of the '90s. Brooks, the committed Revivalist, Ruskin and Morris, are the primary influences and the

116

Century Guild, founded in order '. . . to render all branches of art the sphere no longer of the tradesman, but of the artist . . .' and to 'restore building, decoration, glass painting, pottery, wood-carving and metal to their rightful place beside painting and sculpture', was formed in their image. The Guild's achievements, however, are very different from those of the Firm and its 'style' was determined by new influences. In the first place most of the designers involved in the Guild were some twenty years younger than Morris and his associates. Mackmurdo was thirty-one when he founded it, and Selwyn Image, the co-founder, was thirty-three. (Mackmurdo had met Selwyn Image at Oxford when both were attending Ruskin's drawing school.) Other members of the Guild were younger; Herbert Horne was only eighteen and had joined Mackmurdo as a pupil after two years in a surveyor's office; Clement Heaton, son of the founder of Heaton, Butler and Baynes, stained-glass manufacturers and general decorators, was twenty-one, and Benjamin Creswick, the self-taught sculptor who as a boy had worked in a Sheffield knife factory, was also in his early twenties. Thus the only 'established' designers associated with the Guild at the outset were William De Morgan, who produced tiles for Mackmurdo and Heywood Sumner.

Mackmurdo himself was probably unaware that he was extending the traditions established by Morris; he had new allegiances, to Renaissance architecture, and through his friendships with Whistler and Yeats, to the 'avant-garde' in literature and music. But although he could never claim to belong to Whistler's disciples, that 'youthful élite' who, according to William Rothenstein 'cared little either for Burne-Jones or Morris',[12] he was, like them, reinterpreting and extending the conventions of his art. He visited Italy several times during the 1870s and his sketch books from this period reflect his obsession with the geometry of Renaissance architecture; but they are also filled with naturalistic studies of flowers and plant forms, and Mackmurdo combines these two elements, the structural and the sinuous, in his designs for furniture and fabrics. By this time, too, a seemingly alien element of sophistication had merged with the English craft aesthetic, introduced some twenty years earlier with the discovery of Japan and its artefacts. Although Morris was to maintain that the 'Japanese have no architectural, and therefore no decorative, instinct', and to describe their achievements as 'mere wonderful toys, things quite outside the pale of the evolution of art',[13] many designers from the 1860s onwards were to see in Japanese work a logic, fitness and control that European design lacked. Admittedly, designers such as Christopher Dresser and the architect E. W. Godwin who openly acknowledged their debt to the Japanese stand apart from the Arts and Crafts movement, but their preference for undecorated forms and construction is reflected in Mackmurdo's furniture, as well as that of Voysey and Mackintosh.

The fact that Mackmurdo was involved with an entirely new design aesthetic was apparent in his earliest designs, as well as in the corporate work of the group. The title page of *Wren's City Churches*, for example, which he published in 1883, demonstrates his independence (pl 31). The choice of subject is in itself revealing, and in his unpublished memoirs Mackmurdo describes how 'Morris did his best to put me off by his unmeasured praise of my own constructive work'. For the title page itself

Mackmurdo uses a wood-cut which, in its curious fusion of Blake and the Japanese, has been heralded as a precursor of Art Nouveau. The design is framed with solid columns, and these are flanked by attenuated phoenixes; birds and columns, however, are the only concessions to symmetry, and within this framework the title, on streamers, is set aslant among undulating flame-like flowers, stems and leaves. Similar flame, flower and stem forms appear as elaborate fretwork in the back of a chair that Mackmurdo designed for the Century Guild, perhaps in that same year (pl 27),* and they recur in several of the fabrics and wallpapers produced by the Guild. As with Morris, nature is the source-book—flowers, leaves, animals and birds predominate (Herbert Horne also uses elongated Blake-like figures in his *Angel with the Trumpet*); but although the ingredients are similar, the structure of Century Guild patterns is completely different from that of Morris (pls 34, 36 and 37). Mackmurdo's designs, with their flaring leaves and petals, are almost expressionist in their harshness, vigour and movement; the colours, too—yellow ochres, coral pinks, purples and acid greens, are rarely found in Morris's palette.

Mackmurdo's furniture is less iconoclastic than his pattern-making, and the fret-backed dining chair is probably his most unconventional design. Most of the Century Guild furniture is severe in form, simple and carefully proportioned, perhaps more 'classical' in its detailing than Japanese, although the shaft-like verticals that characterize the work of Godwin, Voysey and above all Mackintosh, are part of Mackmurdo's design idiom. Mahogany, oak and satinwood are the woods most frequently used, and some of the cabinets have painted panels and brass detailing. Although Mackmurdo had made a point of mastering several crafts before he embarked on the Guild venture, not all his designs were executed on the premises; some of the furniture was made by Collinson & Lock, while Jeffrey & Company produced the wallpapers and Simpson & Godlee the fabrics. In producing textiles, furniture, metalware and stained glass, he was following the precedent set by Morris and his Firm; in one important venture, however, the launching of the quarterly magazine *Hobby Horse*, Mackmurdo anticipated Morris. The first issue, edited jointly by Mackmurdo and Herbert Horne, was published in April 1884 with an obsessive line-block cover by Selwyn Image (pl 32). The aim of the magazine, like Cole's some fifty years earlier, was to proclaim the wider aims and ideals of the organization it promoted. 'It became my endeavour', wrote Mackmurdo, 'to add a corner-stone to the work I had started with the formation of the Century Guild of Artists. I might here in this quarterly find a means of reinforcing from season to season the claims of art . . . It sought to encourage and establish a high standard of form and method.'[14]

The *Hobby Horse* was the first of the art-oriented literary magazines of the 1880s and 1890s and it had an eclectic and distinguished list of contributors, including Ruskin, Ford Madox Brown, William Rossetti, G. F. Watts, Burne-Jones, Shields, Oscar Wilde, J. A. Symonds, Arthur Symons and Wilfred Scawen Blunt. It was, as the *Studio* article pointed out, the first magazine to treat 'modern printing . . .

* The chair was illustrated in the *Studio*, April 1899, and dated 1881, by Aymer Vallance; however, since the chair is signed with the Century Guild monogram it must be later in date.

as a serious art', and as such Mackmurdo claims that it made a considerable impression on William Morris (although Morris was obviously already well aware of the problems that Mackmurdo was describing). 'I well remember', writes Mackmurdo in his manuscript, 'showing him a number of the *Hobby Horse* . . . and telling him of the difficulties one had to overcome in getting a page of printed text that was a pleasure to look at; what art there was in proportioning its mass; in setting this text with its nicely proportioned margins upon the page; in the spacing of letters and lines; in the choice of paper, and above all, of available type. The sight of this poor best that by painstaking and taste had been achieved with such material as we had, filled Morris with enthusiasm. He instantly saw what could be done. "Here is a new craft to conquer. A new English type needs to be founded." '

Emery Walker, the *éminence grise* of the private press movement advised Mackmurdo in the initial stages of the *Hobby Horse*, and through his association with the Chiswick Press, supervised the reproduction of the illustrations which were mainly by Image and Horne. The press printed the magazine, which, with its careful layout and typesetting and its handmade paper anticipates the preoccupations of the private presses. Again the *Hobby Horse* was the first magazine to introduce British design and design theory to the Continent; it did not have such a wide circulation as its successor the *Studio*, of course, but it was certainly read by Van de Velde and his associates.* Actual work by the Guild was first exhibited on the Continent in Belgium in 1891, and Horta is reported to have used a Century Guild wallpaper in his Tassel House.[15]

The Guild itself was disbanded in 1888—not apparently for financial reasons, since the group seems to have received a steady stream of commissions, but because its members had begun to concentrate on their own work. Herbert Horne, for example, remained a partner in Mackmurdo's architectural practice until about 1900, but he was becoming increasingly preoccupied with his writing, and he left England to live in Florence in 1900, so that he could write his life of Botticelli. Selwyn Image was also extending both his interests and his reputation: as well as producing designs for embroidery, mosaics and stained glass, he designed a type-face for Macmillans, produced numerous illustrations and published a book of *Poems and Carols* in 1894. He joined the Mackmurdo community in Fitzroy Street in 1898; two years later he was appointed Master of the Art-Workers' Guild and he was Slade Professor of Fine Art at Oxford from 1910 to 1916. Mackmurdo and he maintained their friendship until Image died in 1930.

Clement Heaton, the youngest member of the quartet, became a specialist in cloisonné enamel and established his own firm Cloisonné Mosaics Ltd in the 1880s; he left England in the early '90s to work in Neuchâtel, carrying out several commissions there for stained glass and cloisonné. Later, he patented a process for the manufacture of embossed wallpaper in Switzerland, and he settled in the USA in 1912.

Mackmurdo himself became more and more obsessed with what he called 'the

* Pevsner recounts in his article on Mackmurdo in *Studies in Art, Architecture and Design* (p. 136) how Max Elskamp wrote to Van de Velde describing the second issue of *Van Nu en Straks* as 'vraiment plus beau que le *Hobby Horse*'.

sphere of social politics', and he spent many years attempting to work out a system of economic reform, in which everyone was to be paid in terms of a fixed amount of wheat per day—'which volume', he writes, 'would be equated to the monetary unit or £note'. The Century Guild was his most ambitious experiment, and the one for which he is best known; it was, nevertheless, only one of a series of ventures with which he was associated. During the 1880s, before and while he was involved with the Guild, Mackmurdo had been an active member of several societies. In his autobiography he describes how he had helped to promote Ruskin Societies in London, Birmingham and Manchester; in 1883, a year before the Art-Workers' Guild was established, he organized an exhibition of arts and crafts in Enfield, where he was living, and he was also on the working committee of the Home Arts and Industries Association, whose aim was to revive village handicrafts: 'Many were the artists and art lovers whom we called to this work', he wrote, 'and it grew apace. In 1889 we had 450 classes, about 1,000 teachers and 5,000 students.' He also supported the Fitzroy Picture Society which supplemented the work of the Arts for Schools Association, and he was a founder member of the National Association for the Advancement of Art and its Application to Industry, whose work will be discussed later.

The Art-Workers' Guild

Mackmurdo claims, in his memoirs, that the Century Guild 'gave birth to the Art-Workers' Guild'; but this organization, which was founded in 1884, brought together several groups of architect/craftsmen who looked on Ruskin and Morris as their spiritual fathers. The initial impetus for the formation of a 'guild of Handicraftsmen and Designers in the Arts' came from a group of Norman Shaw's pupils and assistants who in 1883 began to hold monthly meetings in order to discuss art and architecture. Prominent among them was William Lethaby, who had been with Shaw for the past five years, and who during his apprenticeship in his native Barnstaple had designed farm buildings that 'had to work efficiently as an engine or a pump does'.[16] The principal preoccupations of the St George's Society,* as the group called itself, concerned the breakdown of relations between the artist, the architect and the craftsman; they felt that the isolationist policy of the Royal Academy and what they called the commercialism and the 'professionalism' of the Institute of British Architects, were destroying the essential unity of the arts, and they began to investigate a means of bringing together those 'who were neither the oil painters of the Academy nor the Surveyors of the Institute, but craftsmen in architecture, painting, sculpture and the kindred arts'.[17] Norman Shaw gave them his encouragement, and a circular was distributed among artists and craftsmen inviting them to a meeting at the Charing Cross Hotel. The number who met there in January 1884 was twenty-five, a substantial lobby being provided by a group calling itself the 'Fifteen' which had been launched four years earlier on the initiative of Lewis F. Day.

* The group took its name from the nearby Bloomsbury Church, and there was, apparently, no reference implied to Ruskin's Guild.

Lewis Day was a prolific writer of textbooks on ornament and pattern (titles include *The Anatomy of Pattern*, *The Planning of Ornament*, *Nature in Ornament*, etc). He had specialized as a designer of stained glass until 1870 when he had formed his own firm. In this capacity he designed textiles (see pl 65), wallpapers, carpets, tiles, pottery, clocks and some furniture, and in 1881 he was appointed Art Director of Turnbull & Stockdale, who produced fabrics. He was, therefore, a successful designer for the 'trade', and at the same time was a perceptive critic and observer of contemporary design practice (his essay 'William Morris and his Art' in the *Art Journal*'s Easter Art Annual for 1899 is still worth reading as a sound, objective and well-balanced assessment of Morris's achievements). Other members of the 'Fifteen' included Walter Crane, Henry Holiday, T. M. Rooke, G. T. Robinson, John Sedding, George Simonds and Hugh Stannus, and, according to Crane, they met in each other's houses from May to October in order 'to provide a paper or open a discussion on some subject or question of decorative art'.[18] Most of the 'Fifteen' became members of the Art-Workers' Guild from the outset, and many of them subsequently became Masters.

The Guild, therefore, provided a focus for a growing number of artists, architects and designers who were attempting to extend and redefine their professional attitudes and status. Some of its members hoped that the organization might provide an influential alternative to the two professional bodies, the Royal Academy and the Institute of British Architects, but from its outset there were conflicting attitudes concerning the public rôle of the Guild, which over the years became more of a private club and artistic 'lodge' for the interchange of ideas and opinions than a fighting body dedicated to the promotion of its ideals and its members. (British designers had, in fact, to wait until 1930 for the formation of their professional body—the Society of Industrial Artists.) The decision to avoid publicity, taken in all good faith, meant that the Guild's influence was subtle rather than overt, and in the end it was its 'off-shoot' —the Arts and Crafts Exhibition Society—that succeeded in promoting the native craft ideals and achievement at an international level. Massé's history of the first half-century of the Guild demonstrates the dissensions that the numerous decisions to avoid public controversy caused among members. The first major crisis came in 1890 when Hugh Stannus, Christopher Whall and Selwyn Image formed a sub-committee to report on the question of the control of advertisements, and their report, in favour of Guild action, was rejected by the majority of members. John Brett, the Master for that year, expressed his disgust in his address to the Guild:

'The project was smothered, and this, the first opportunity that the Guild had of doing great public service, was thrown away . . . Thus we see the spectacle of a Guild, which, though comprising within its fold a large selection from the rising artistic talent of the day, yet has so little of definite purpose that it confirms the worst that has been said of the unbusinesslike character of the artistic temperament. When a great opportunity for practical effort arises, it hastens precipitately to conceal itself.'[19]

The Guild, however, steadfastly refused to give itself a public face; in 1897 and 1899 the rules against 'pledging the Guild to public action' were tightened. Nor were its members eager for personal publicity. Grant Richards's suggestion in 1899 that an illustrated *Year Book of the Guild* should be produced was rejected as 'quite foreign to the traditions of the Guild'; the idea that a special issue of the *Studio* should be devoted to work of its members was 'absolutely repugnant' and when in 1901 *The Artist* suggested that it should be appointed 'official organ and mouthpiece of the Guild', its editor was told that the Guild 'had systematically avoided any such publicity'.[20]

In the words of H. Wilson, Master for 1917, the Guild was, for its members 'a spiritual oasis in the wilderness of modern life'; nevertheless it was a unique body and its influence, though concealed, was powerful:

'There is no competition, since there is no comparison, with other and similar societies, for there are none similar. We do not strive towards a definite material end. We neither seek public recognition, nor try to teach the world, nor even, definitely to teach each other; yet we are not without aims. Each member learns from each . . . So ultimately, we do teach the world and give our Professors of Art to the Ancient Universities, our Architects to be custodians of great cathedrals, our painters and sculptors to the Royal Academy, leaders and teachers to every craft and School of crafts.'[21]

The speaker here was Edward Warren, Master in 1913, and he was quite correct in his assertion that membership of the Guild, which was by election among its members, was in itself a recommendation for positions of authority and responsibility. Walter Crane, for example, who had been president both of the Guild and the Arts and Crafts Exhibition Society, was appointed director of design at the Manchester Municipal School of Art in 1893; he became art director of Reading University College in 1896 and principal of the Royal College of Art in 1898. William Lethaby and George Frampton were joint principals of the LCC Central School of Arts and Crafts when it was founded in 1896, drawing their staff from among members of the Guild; R. Catterson-Smith was headmaster of the Birmingham Central School, Edward Prior was Slade Professor of Fine Art at Cambridge in 1912, and both Anning Bell and Caley Robinson taught at the Glasgow School of Art. The Guild, therefore, was a powerful force in the promotion of Arts and Crafts ideals in education, and its meetings and lectures provided a useful platform for the interchange of ideas and theory.

It is, however, interesting to speculate whether members of the Guild would have been able to claim such prestige and influence had not other organizations assumed the task of publicizing the ideals and achievements of the 'art-worker' movement.

The Arts and Crafts Exhibition Society

The Arts and Crafts Exhibition Society provided a platform for demonstrating not only the work of the movement but the philosophy that lay behind it. The idea of a continuing series of public exhibitions devoted to the applied arts, was, of course, not a new one. In the earlier part of the century the Royal Society of Arts had begun to fulfil that rôle, and the great trade exhibitions following 1851 were in part the consequence of the society's concern with design and manufacture. To the artist/craftsman, however, there were obvious limitations in the commercial approach; what was needed was a selective display that carried the prestige of the Royal Academy's annual exhibition, and throughout the century pressure was brought to bear on that august body to open its doors to the applied arts (a pressure that had its counterpart in the various 'Secession' movements on the Continent). Many of the original members had joined the Art-Workers' Guild on the assumption that it would sponsor exhibitions. This had, in fact, been a fundamental premise of the St George's Art Society group, and at the original meeting to discuss the formation of a new society Ernest Newton presented a scheme for an 'Association with Exhibitions, recruiting itself from the body of the Exhibitors', while Lethaby had suggested 'the institution of a National Gallery of Representative Modern Painting and Sculpture . . . permanent collections . . . and loan exhibitions'.[22] When it became obvious that the Guild would not sponsor corporate action of this kind, a splinter group was formed in 1886, its most prominent members being Walter Crane, Heywood Sumner, W. A. S. Benson, T. J. Cobden-Sanderson, William De Morgan, Lewis Day and Lethaby. Benson, a friend of Morris, who had trained as an architect and had then specialized in metalwork, circulated a scheme for an exhibition under the title 'The Combined Arts', a committee was formed under the chairmanship of Walter Crane, and in November 1888 the society held its first exhibition in the New Gallery in Regent Street.

The term 'Arts and Crafts' was therefore first used in connection with this society— the phrase being coined apparently by T. J. Cobden-Sanderson to replace the clumsy 'combined arts' nomenclature. In its early years the society fulfilled all the aspirations of its members and, in fact, achieved a prestige far beyond their hopes. Before the group was founded, fears had been expressed for it on commercial as well as aesthetic grounds, and to the consternation of some of its members, William Morris was among the most sceptical. As well as voicing very practical doubts as to the financial viability of the scheme, Morris was, by this time, becoming more inclined to leave the battle for design reform to younger enthusiasts, and was in any case growing more and more convinced of the futility of corporate effort in a capitalist society. According to Mackail, Morris thought that the society's campaign to credit the craftsman/maker, as well as the designer of the work exhibited, was a 'trivial one', and that 'it was not by printing lists of names in a catalogue that the status of the workman could be raised, or the system of capitalistic commerce altered in the slightest degree'. In a letter about the society's aims, also quoted by Mackail, he wrote: 'One thing will have to be made clear . . . ie, who is to find the money . . . the general public don't care a damn about the arts and crafts, and our customers can come to our shops to look at our kind of goods.'[23] He also expressed a fear, shared by some of the anti-exhibition lobby within the guild, that, apart from a few outstanding designs, the work would 'tend to be of an amateurish nature'.

In the event, however, these fears were only half-justified, for although the society was unable to support an annual exhibition, its activities enjoyed a growing prestige, both in Britain and abroad, and as well as enabling members to mount displays of goods selected according to agreed standards of design and craftsmanship, the lectures and publications associated with the society gave them an opportunity to define these standards. Predictably enough, both the aesthetic and the philosophy are derived from Ruskin and Morris; Walter Crane, the society's first president, writing on 'The Revival of Design and Handicraft' in the *Arts and Craft Essays*[24] set the context of their activities in Morrisian terms: 'The movement . . . represents in some sense a revolt against the hard mechanical conventional life and its insensibility to beauty (quite another thing to ornament). It is a protest against that so-called industrial progress which provides shoddy wares, the cheapness of which is paid for by the lives of their producers and the degradation of their users.'

Walter Crane

Crane, himself a dedicated socialist in the Morris tradition, is probably best known today as an illustrator of children's books. His first employer was Edmund Evans, and in his book *An Artist's Reminiscences* he describes how he was 'in the habit of putting in all sorts of subsidiary details that interested me and often made them the vehicle for my ideas in furniture and decoration'. He designed his first wallpapers for Metford Warner of Jeffrey & Co in 1875, and his connection with this firm was to last for thirty years. But as well as designing wallpapers, he designed textiles, carpets and ceramics, and by the 1880s was considered one of the leading figures of the aesthetic movement, his work being highly praised on the Continent. For, in spite of his condemnation of the 'decadent influence' of Art Nouveau, and in spite of his reservations about Japanese art, whose impact, he maintained, had 'been to loosen the restraining and architectonic sense of balance and fitness and a definite ordered plan of construction, which are essential in the finest types of design',[25] Crane produced work that can be defined as Art Nouveau. Where he uses leaves, flowers and plant forms, his designs are full of movement, tender and lyrical: his work has none of the harshness or vigour of, say, a Mackmurdo or a Dresser. As well as these naturalistic motifs, Crane introduces Pre-Raphaelite inspired knights and ladies, strange beasts and exotic birds in his designs, and although the repeats are carefully controlled the effect is one of asymmetry, complexity and movement. His patterns, unlike those of Morris and Voysey, are 'graphic' rather than architectural, and it was this essentially linear quality, this subtlety and suppleness of line that appealed to Continental designers. Schmutzler in his superb book *Art Nouveau* maintains that in the 1890s Crane was 'the most popular Morris pupil and representative of the Pre-Raphaelitism throughout the Continent' and the Crane 'cult' was furthered by designer/theorists such as Lemmen, who published a detailed analysis of his work in 1891. Van de Velde, writing about wallpapers in *L'Art Moderne* in 1893 also singled out Crane for especial praise and quoted from his introductory essays in the Arts and Crafts publication of

78 Tooled leather wall-covering in Ashbee's house, *Magpie and Stump*, which was decorated throughout by the Guild of Handicraft as a demonstration of their skills *c.* 1894

79 Silver bowl, embossed and chased with a leaf design; cast legs. Designed by C. R. Ashbee and made by the Guild of Handicraft, *c.* 1893 *Victoria and Albert Museum*

opposite

80 Ciborium, designed by C. R. Ashbee and made for St Aidan's Church, Birmingham, by the Guild of Handicraft, 1909. Silver, set with amethysts *The Worshipful Company of Gold-smiths.*

81 Silver cup designed by the Guild of Handicraft and made by C. R. Ashbee, 1901-2 *Victoria and Albert Museum*

opposite
82 The 'Painter - Stainers' Cup'; silver, set with semi-precious stones. Designed by C. R. Ashbee
c. 1900. *Victoria and Albert Museum*

83 Cutlery, designed by C. R. Ashbee and made by the Guild of Handicraft, 1900-2 *Victoria and Albert Museum*

FAREWELL AND ADIEU. Seamen's traditional.

Farewell and Adieu, all you fine Spanish ladies:
    Farewell and Adieu, all you ladies of Spain;
For we're under orders to sail for old England,
    And perhaps we may never more see you again.
Chorus. We'll rant and we'll roar like true British sailors,
        We'll range and we'll roam over all the salt seas,
        Until we strike soundings in the Channel of England:
        From Ushant to Scilly 'tis thirty-five leagues.

We hove our ship to when the wind was sou'-west, boys,
    We hove our ship to for to strike soundings clear;
Then we filled our main-topsail and bore right away, boys, °
    And away up the Channel our course we did steer.
Chorus. We'll rant, &c.

The first land we made it is known as the Deadman,
    Next Ram Head near Plymouth, Start, Portland, & Wight;
We sailed past Beachy, past Fairly and Dungeness,
    And then bore away for the South Foreland Light.
Chorus. We'll rant, &c.

Then the signal was made for the grand fleet to anchor,
    All, all in the Downs that night for to meet;
So stand by your stoppers: see clear your shank-painters;
    Haul all your clue-garnets, stick out tacks and sheets.
Chorus. We'll rant, &c.

Now let every man toss off a full bumper,
    Now let every man toss off a full bowl;
For we will be jolly and drown melancholy
    With a health to each jovial and true-hearted soul.
Chorus. We'll rant, &c.
                                        bottom.
° Alternative line: There was forty-five fathoms & a clear sandy
    II.—4

THEY WHO TO STATES AND GOVERNOURS OF THE COMMONWEALTH DIRECT THEIR SPEECH, HIGH COURT OF PARLAMENT,

or wanting such accesse in a private condition, write that which they foresee may advance the publick good; I suppose them as at the beginning of no meane endeavour, not a little alter'd & mov'd inwardly in their mindes: Some with doubt of what will be the successe, others with feare of what will be the censure; some with hope, others with confidence of what they have to speake. And me perhaps each of these dispositions, as the subject was whereon I enter'd, may have at other times variously affected; & likely might in these formost expressions now also disclose which of them sway'd most, but that the very attempt of this addresse thus made, and the thought of whom it hath recourse to, hath got the power within me to a passion, farre more welcome then incidentall to a Preface. Which though I stay not to confesse ere any aske, I shall be blamelesse, if it be no other, then the joy & gratulation which it brings to all who wish and promote their Countries liberty; whereof this whole Discourse propos'd will be a certaine testimony, if not a Trophey. For this is not the liberty which wee can hope, that no grievance ever should arise in the Commonwealth, that let no man in this

8

87 Tea service and cutlery designed by Henry van de Velde for Th. Müller, Weimar; reproduced from the 1912 *Werkbund Jahrbuch*

88 Chair, designed by M. H. Baillie-Scott and made by the Guild of Handicraft for the Palace of Darmstadt, *c.* 1898 *Victoria and Albert Museum*

89 Coffee pot, designed by Richard Riemerschmid for the *Hellerau Werkstätte;* reproduced from the 1914 *Werkbund Jahrbuch*

opposite

90 Linoleum designed for the Delmenhorster-Fabrik, Anker-Marke. Top: Josef Hoffmann; bottom: Henry van de Velde. Reproduced from the 1912 *Werkbund Jahrbuch*

91 Wash set for hotel use, designed by Adelbert Niemeyer for Villeroy and Boch, Munich. Reproduced from the 1914 *Werkbund Jahrbuch*

92 Cabin for the *Kronprinzessin Cecilie* designed by Richard Riemerschmid; reproduced from the 1914 *Werkbund Jahrbuch*

93 Locomotive illustrated in the 1914 *Werkbund Jahrbuch;* designed and made by the Maschinenfabrik, Esslingen, Wurttemberg

94 Detail of car, designed by Ernst Neumann and reproduced from the 1914 *Werkbund Jahrbuch*

95 Sideboard in walnut with ebony handles; designed by Gordon Russell, and made by Gordon Russell Ltd, *c.* 1928

96 Waxed oak table designed by Ambrose Heal and made by Heal & Son Ltd, *c.* 1922

97 Earthenware dish and mug, made by A. W. Finch at the 'Iris' Workshops, 1900 *Victoria and Albert Museum*

98

99

98 Stoneware vase designed by Wilhelm Kåge for Gustavsberg, 1953 *Victoria and Albert Museum*

99 Collapsible deckchair in teak and wicker, designed by Kaare Klint, 1933 *Victoria and Albert Museum*

100 Birch laminate chair, designed by Alvar Aalto for Artek, *c.* 1929 *Victoria and Albert Museum*

32.

that same year; and, again in 1893 Crane's book *The Claims of Decorative Art* was translated into Dutch, when it was redesigned with illustrations by G. W. Dijsselhof, and retitled, significantly, *Art and the Community*. Today, Crane's work as a theorist has been eclipsed by that of Morris, whose ideals he faithfully repeats; but at the same time Crane obviously made a formidable impression on his contemporaries, as a teacher, as well as designer and theorist. *The Claims of Decorative Art* had been published in 1892, the year before his appointment to Manchester, and in this book he had pleaded for spontaneity rather than systems, instinct rather than rule, subjectivity rather than objectivity, for he was convinced that 'there is nothing absolute in art. *Art is not Science.*' This, of course, implied a criticism of the South Kensington régime, and in his teaching at Manchester, Crane attempted to introduce 'new methods with the existing curriculum'.[26] *The Claims of Decorative Art* was followed by *The Bases of Design* in 1898, and in 1900 Crane published *Line and Form*, a re-exploration of his attitudes to design.

Crane spent only a year as Principal of the Royal College of Art—his appointment was in 1898, two years after the Kensington School had been designated with that title, and had been permitted to grant its own diploma. He found, when he took over, that the college was 'run as a sort of mill in which to prepare art teachers', and that the staff, although eager to please, had been 'hardened by long service in a system with which I was out of sympathy'.[27] Before he resigned, however, Crane had succeeded in revolutionizing the system of instruction. There were, he maintained, two systems of education in art.

'i   The Academic or absolute
ii The Experimental or relative, and adaptive

The one teaching art and design in the abstract on certain cut-and-dried principles and methods, and fixed canons and standards, passing every mind through the same mill, without special reference to any particular conditions of craftsmanship or individual preference. The other teaching design in concrete forms, and in direct relation to tools, methods and materials, with the object of calling out the individual feeling and setting it free to express itself under the natural limitations of art in its own way.'[28]

The second way was the method adopted by the reformed Arts and Crafts schools, and during Crane's brief control of the college he introduced Art-Workers' Guild members and methods to the college—Alexander Fisher for enamelling, Cobden-Sanderson for book-binding and Joseph Pennell for book-illustration. In 1899 Crane became a member of the newly formed Council of Advice on Art, and in 1901 the college, on its recommendations, was reorganized into four main schools: design, under Lethaby, architecture under Beresford Pite, painting under Gerald Moira and sculpture under E. Lanteri. All were members of the Art-Workers' Guild, as were many of their staff, who included Christopher Whall, Edward Johnston, Henry Wilson and George Jack. In each case the student was taught mastery of a craft; neither Crane nor the teachers he promoted believed in 'cast-iron systems'. Education, according to Crane 'must be varied according to the individual. It must be made personal and interesting or it is of little good . . .' But at the same time Crane believed that the curriculum, to be valid, must work within a wider context, since the purpose of the new courses was 'to further the advancement of art in its application to industry'.[29]

By this time Arts and Crafts relationships with industry, which will be discussed in the next chapter, were changing. The designers still maintained their missionary rôle, but the sympathetic manufacturer was now considered worthy of conversion and collaboration. The overtures, needless to say, were in most cases tentative, a common language failed to emerge, and in the end the reformed and liberalized art schools proved as ineffective and as incapable of producing industrial designers as their predecessors. But for a brief period at the turn of the century, some sections of British industry did succeed in establishing standards that embraced the craft aesthetic.

5 Guildsmen and industry

The craft aesthetic, as we have seen, was concerned with fitness and propriety; it demanded that materials and function should determine the design solution, and because nature expressed herself in a multitude of exquisite shapes, forms and colours, it permitted what Morris might have called 'the blossoms of the art of design' in textiles, furniture, metalware and ceramics. These assumptions concerning the nature of the design process were fundamental to nineteenth-century design philosophy, as it developed in England, and they had been formulated long before the Arts and Crafts movement appropriated them and associated with them the especial virtues of handwork. In the early part of the century, however, when a general concern for design standards was first being expressed, such ideals were considered appropriate to both craft and machine production, and, in fact, little attempt was made to distinguish between the two. The Select Committee of 1835, for example, heard evidence from artists, educationists and manufacturers, and it also invited James Nasmyth, the distinguished engineer, to act as witness. He was asked how he would carry into effect 'the combination of beauty of design with machinery', and, in the light of later critics' reactions to the excesses of the Great Exhibition, his reply is significant: 'I would show', he stated, 'the means of combining the most beautiful forms and the most scientific applications of materials employed in the formation of machinery with the greatest economy. In the majority of instances, the most economic deposition of materials coincides with such form as presents the most elegant appearance to the eye.'

One tends to associate the conviction that functional efficiency will impose its own form and that the result will be inherently beautiful with early twentieth-century theory. The idea, however, with its platonic associations, was fundamental nineteenth-century theory, and was clearly expressed in criticisms arising from the Great Exhibition. Gottfried Semper, for example, found little to inspire him among the exhibits he saw there, but he did admire the coaches, weapons and medical equipment and praised these for their sound *functional* design. Richard Redgrave expressed a similar point of view, and his *Supplementary Report on Design* described how the indiscriminate use of ornamentation 'is apt to sicken us of decoration, and lead us to admire those objects of absolute utility (the machines and utensils of various kinds) where use is so paramount that ornament is repudiated, and fitness of purpose being the end sought, a noble simplicity is the result'. The theme was also reiterated in *The Times*; in the article already quoted in Chapter 1, the anonymous correspondent wrote:

'The most refined taste might have gathered pleasure and satisfaction from our machinery department . . . The only beauty attempted was that which the stringent application to mechanical science to the material world could supply; and in the truthfulness, perseverance, and severity with which that idea was carried out, there developed a style of art at once national and grand.'

This severe, truthful, austere and seemingly national style continued to be expressed in the engineering achievements of the nineteenth century, but the idea that the basis of a new *aesthetic* might be found there was never fully formulated, and as has been already pointed out, Britain failed to produce an adequate prophet of technique and functionalism. Although there were several critics ready to point to the inadequacies of his reasoning,[1] the ethics of Ruskin prevailed, and as the idea that the engineer could produce 'art' grew less and less acceptable, the campaign for design reform was concentrated on certain well-defined sections of industry. By the 1870s, it seems, the divorce was complete, and in this context the title of the international exhibition held in Paris in 1878—Great Exhibition of Works of Art and Art Industry—is significant. The *Art Journal*,[2] that infallible guide to establishment attitudes in matters of taste, approved of this specialization. 'The heavy and ruder productions of industry have intense interest for the scientific, the commercial and the economical worlds', declared their catalogue, 'but it is the mass of beautiful works, in which Art and handicraft are happily blended, that attracts and delights not only the adept and the connoisseur, but also those who merely admire beauty and novelty'.

By this time 'Art' had become a powerful incentive to sales in international markets, and it was generally accepted by the more successful practitioners in the semi-craft industries, such as pottery, glass, furniture, textiles, etc, that their products should be 'designed', and that consultants and specialists should be used for this purpose. Morris's Firm, the Century Guild and the Arts and Crafts designers were part of this phenomenon. As far as textiles were concerned, Morris was the only designer to make a consistent attempt to carry out his own production; the rest, like Voysey, worked for established manufacturers, and in other fields too their ideas were absorbed and imitated by industry—a fact that was noted by Walter Crane, who, in an essay on the *Arts and Crafts Movement*[3] quoted, approvingly, a trade journal review of an Exhibition Society display: 'The arts and crafts movement', stated the reviewer, 'has been the best influence upon machine industry during the past ten years . . . while we have sought to develop handicraft beside it on sound and independent lines, we have succeeded in imparting something of the spirit of craftsmanship to the best kind of machine-work, bridging over the former gulf between machinery and tools, and quickening machine industry with a new sense of the artistic possibilities that lie within its proper sphere.' And this, according to Crane, was an acceptable compromise, for he comments:

'The organised factory and the great machine industries will continue to work for the million, as well as for the millionaire, under the present system of production; but, at any rate, they can be influenced by ideas of design, and it must be said that some manufacturers have shown themselves fully alive to the value of the co-operation of artists in this direction.'[4]

Pottery

During the 1870s several leading pottery manufacturers had begun to produce, alongside their commercial ranges, 'Art' pottery which appealed to more refined tastes: Mintons, for example, opened their Art-Pottery Studios in South Kensington in 1871; the studios were supplied with biscuit pottery from the factory in Stoke, and the pieces were then decorated individually by various artists.

Howell & James, whose representatives had testified to the Select Committee of 1835, and who by the 1860s and '70s were specializing in both the production and retailing of 'Art Manufactures' also took pottery from established makers and organized competitions for its embellishment. Their 'paintings on porcelain' were much admired in the 1878 Paris exhibition, and the *Art Journal* catalogue approved of their 'happy idea' of encouraging amateur talent, since it 'directed the attention of ladies to an employment at once pleasant and remunerative, giving, or rather extending occupation for women—a social requirement universally admitted'.

More in keeping, however, with the nascent ideals of the Arts and Crafts movement, was Doulton's collaboration with the Lambeth School of Art. This began in the 1860s when Henry Doulton, who was on the committee of the School, became friendly with J. C. L. Sparkes, its headmaster. As a result of this friendship and his general interest in the School, Doulton decided to revive the production of saltglazed stoneware; this had formed the bulk of the firm's output when it was first established in Lambeth in 1815, but it had been superseded in popularity by the more refined developments in earthenware and bone china. Doulton resolved, however, with the collaboration of the students, to reintroduce a more sophisticated variant of this ware. It must be noted, however, that this was not 'craft' pottery in the contemporary sense; Doultons supplied the throwers and the turners, and the students selected from available shapes and experimented with various methods of surface decoration. The results were charming and highly individualistic, and a handful of the Doulton 'designers' including the Barlow family (Hannah, Florence and Arthur), Emily Edwards, Frank Butler and George Tinworth, became well known for their work. The ware was first shown to the public at the International Exhibition of 1871, when George Wallis, Keeper of the Art Collections at South Kensington, deemed the decoration 'thoroughly well considered and especially adapted to the material, the mode of production and the use of the object'. And in spite of the 'division of labour' Wallis praised the unity of form and decoration that resulted from the collaboration of craftsmen and artists. 'When colour is introduced', he wrote, 'it is done sparingly, and with a view to enhance the form of the object and the natural beauty of the material, rather than to conceal the one or the other.'[5]

The four Martin brothers, however, Lambeth's most celebrated students, overcame this distinction between the 'artist' and the 'craftsman', and worked in London for almost forty years as a unique 'potters' collaborative'. The eldest, Wallace, had trained as a sculptor, and began his career as a sculptor's assistant in the Houses of Parliament. He began to attend evening classes at the Lambeth Art School in the 1860s, and together with George Tinworth, one of Doulton's designers, entered the Royal Academy Schools in 1864. He appears to have decided to specialize in pottery rather than sculpture during the early 1870s, since he worked at potteries in Devon and Staffordshire, as well as C. J. C. Bailey's Fulham Pottery, before the family concern was established in Fulham in 1873. His three brothers had all attended the Lambeth School at various stages, and they worked with him so successfully that they moved to a larger and more convenient site in Southall in 1877, and two years later opened a shop near High Holborn. Although they were each capable of undertaking the various processes involved, each tended to concentrate on his own specialization. Wallace, the head of the firm, was the modeller; Charles acted as business manager and was responsible for the shop; Walter was the thrower, and he also supervised the kilns and the production processes, while Edwin, the youngest, was the decorator. Since the firm survived until 1914, their output was varied and extensive, and although they concentrated on stoneware, there were several changes of style. In the 1870s, for example, the jugs and vases were perhaps somewhat crude in shape, and were encrusted with vigorous relief patterns, mainly geometric in origin; during the '80s the shapes became more subtle, brown earth colours replaced the blues and greys of the earlier production and the decoration became less obsessive, the geometric patterning giving way to leaves and plant forms (pls 42 and 43). In the later years the brothers experimented with various shapes and surface textures; some of the vases were produced in simple ribbed forms, reminiscent of gourds, while others were decorated with strange fish and dragons, and asymmetrically placed leaf and flower forms. Wallace was responsible, however, for the grotesque birds and 'face' jugs for which the firm is now perhaps best known (pl 55). He began to design his birds, wordly wise with their self-important beaks, emphatic webbed feet and evil claws in the early 1880s; the face jugs came later and both types were obviously produced until the last days of the firm, since a photograph of 1910 shows Walter and Edwin working on simple vase shapes while Wallace is attended by his more eccentric production—brothers and birds showing a remarkable similarity of expression (pl 45).

This growing demand for more personal design led to a renewed interest in local craft pottery, such as that produced at Rye, and to the establishment of several small craft-based concerns, whose aim was to produce 'art' pottery, and whose output provided an alternative to the products of Stoke-on-Trent. In 1879, for example, Henry Tooth took charge of a pottery that had recently been established at Linthorpe, near Middlesbrough, and he invited Christopher Dresser, who was by then well known as a designer and a theorist, to act as art adviser. Dresser was also associated with the Bretby Art Pottery which Tooth set up with his new partner, William Ault, in 1883, and with Ault's own pottery at Swadlincote, which flourished in the late 1880s and early 1890s. Dresser's pottery, like his metalwork, is powerful and idiosyncratic; he believed that 'the first aim of the designer of any article must be to render the object that he produces useful',[6] and at the same time he had a more mystical view of his art, admiring the 'power, energy, force or vigour' that he saw in the 'bursting buds of Spring', 'the spring growth of a luxurious tropical vegetation', 'those forms to be seen in certain bones of birds which are associated with the organs of flight', and in the 'grotesques' of ancient cultures[7]. These preoccupations are reflected in his pottery, much of which seems inspired by pre-Columbian work, and has a harsh, vigorous, primitive quality totally alien to contemporary production.

More in keeping with accepted 'aesthetic' principles and highly regarded in Arts and Crafts as well as aristocratic circles, was the Della Robbia pottery which Harold Rathbone, a painter and a former pupil of Madox Brown, established in Birkenhead in 1894; Rathbone, whose impressions of Madox Brown are quoted in Hueffer's *Record*,[8] thought his master a man in the same mould as 'Shakespeare, Homer, Dante and Hogarth'. 'Whatever artistic and practical success I have had with the Della Robbia pottery', he wrote, 'I attribute mainly to his influence, and I consider it constantly a duty to hand on those traditions to my pupils.' His pottery survived until 1906, a period of trade depression that was to be fatal to other members of the Arts and Crafts movement, including Ashbee and William De Morgan.

William De Morgan, both in his career, and in his attitudes to the design and production of pottery, epitomizes all the strength and weakness of the Arts and Crafts movement. The impetus for his work came from the ideal of the artist as craftsman; his approach was totally individualistic, and like Morris, he went back to first principles in order to achieve the richness and elaboration he required. Although at the end of his career he became better known as a novelist than as a craftsman, he rarely wrote about his work,[9] and Blunt's *The Wonderful Village*[10] remains the best contemporary evocation of his ideals and frustrations. But at the same time he weaves his way into the records and recollections of the period; he knew Rossetti and Burne-Jones, and through his work for the Firm became a lifelong friend of the Morris family; he was associated with Mackmurdo's Century Guild, and Ashbee, in his memoirs, always writes about him with affection and concern: 'With his delightful blue eyes and his brazil nut shaped head, a sort of curly tuft upon it, his musical high pitched voice, he is a most likeable man'.[11] But although he worked for the Firm in its early days, went 'factory' hunting with Morris and moved his workshops to Merton Abbey, near Morris, in 1882, De Morgan preferred to remain independent. He took on partners, associates and craftsmen, he supplied Morris & Co. with tiles, but he never formed, or joined a 'collaborative', and it was probably due to his individualism as much as to his ill-health and financial problems, that he was one of the few well-known designers of his generation who was not a member of the Art-Workers' Guild. 'I could never work', he wrote, 'except by myself and in my own manner.'[12]

De Morgan was born in 1839, and his father, who was of French extraction, was a well-known mathematician. William went to the Royal Academy Schools when he was twenty, and it was during the early sixties that he first got to know Morris and his circle. His first work as a craftsman was in stained glass, and it was not until the 1870s when he moved with his widowed mother and sister to Cheyne Row, Chelsea, that he began to decorate tiles and pottery. From the start, as was predictable with a stained-glass designer, he was preoccupied with colour, pattern and surface texture, and he began experimenting with his lustre and his Persian colours during the Chelsea decade. At first he often bought factory-made tiles in their biscuit state and he also decorated standard unglazed shapes from the Staffordshire potteries; however, in spite of the fact that some of his facilities were somewhat limited he did produce some hand-made ware during the Chelsea period. After the move to Merton, when he had the space to expand and to install larger kilns, he was able to extend both his staff and his output. In his lustre ware he revived a decorative technique which, at that time, was perhaps considered somewhat old-fashioned, but in his attempts to achieve and surpass the best work of the past he created designs that had no parallel; similarly in his 'Persian' ware, he could produce tiles that almost exactly matched the originals, but at the same time he worked in a way that was entirely his own. An interesting corroboration of his preoccupation with age-old techniques is given in Ashbee's memoirs. In 1918 Ashbee went to Palestine as a civic adviser, and in this capacity he was concerned with the revival of various crafts, among them tile-making. Armenian potters, who still worked according to traditional methods, were brought in, and Ashbee sent for plans of De Morgan's kilns and thirty crates of his ware. 'I gave them to Ohanessian, the Armenian', he writes. 'He brought back the plans in great excitement. "But this is wonderful. This is a medieval pattern of a furnace construction we abandoned in Kutahia, for the better sixteenth-century construction we use now. How *did* you come by it?" Then I told him how De Morgan had once said to me he had rediscovered the art of pottery from the beginning.'[13]

This absorption with authenticity, however, did not ensure De Morgan's financial success; while he was at Merton he continued to live in Chelsea and he kept up his showroom in London. The strain of maintaining and commuting between the two establishments was too much for him, and in 1888 he gave up Merton and set up the Sands End Pottery in Fulham with Halsey Ricardo. During the early 1890s, however, his health forced him to spend his winters in Florence, and in 1898 the partnership with Ricardo, who was becoming increasingly successful as an architect, was dissolved (although he still continued to work with Ricardo, supplying tiles for Sir Ernest Debenham's fantastic house at 8 Addison Rd, Kensington). From then on De Morgan's craftsmen partners, Fred and Charles Passenger, and Frank Iles, were responsible for the day-to-day running of the pottery, although De Morgan's method of designing his 'Persian' tile patterns ensured that he retained control over this aspect of his work. He painted his patterns on paper, and sent them to his 'painters', who then traced them, also on to paper, using the same type of brushes as De Morgan to fill in the outlines; the papers were then placed on the tiles, which were covered with a ground of porcelain slip; a light covering of raw glaze was added and the tiles were fired. In the process the paper was destroyed, but the paint was fused into the white ground. This method was used for De Morgan's large picture panels, and it also enabled him to send patterns from Florence, where he employed Italian designers.[14]

But in spite of his ingenuity, and the support of craftsmen who had been with him virtually throughout his career as a potter, De Morgan was forced for economic reasons to close his pottery in 1907. There was an attempt, with the Passengers, to continue the work with Ashbee, but as he was also faced with a financial crisis the plans did not develop; Ashbee records, however, how he told the sad story of De Morgan to an audience in Rhode Island, whereupon a wealthy American lady offered to save the pottery if De Morgan would agree to set it up in Providence. This De Morgan refused to do, saying that the Americans would only use his name and mess up his work. The Passengers, according to Ashbee, were interested in the idea; by the time they had worked out their plans, however, the lady's heirs had got wind of the scheme, persuaded her that there were better things she could do with her money.[15]

De Morgan died in 1917, having achieved during the last ten years of his life latter-day fame and no little fortune as a novelist. The cheques rolled in, but as De Morgan pointed out, they would have been more welcome had they arrived in time to save the pottery. 'All my life', he said, 'I have been trying to make beautiful things, and now that I am able to make them, nobody wants them. Only my extinction can make them valuable.'[16]

This, of course, is the traditional fate of artists, and although in the nineteenth century many of them managed to live very well indeed, the conviction remained, especially among the designer/craftsmen, that they must maintain a united front against the onslaughts of the Philistines. And the fact that many of these Philistines professed to love and foster 'Art' only made matters worse, since their conception of the artist's rôle in society was very different from that of those who sought to refine and reform the taste of their contemporaries. The new patrons, it was felt, were too eager for novelty and display, and they could not be made to understand that art was an expression of life, and that the true artist must be concerned with truth and humanity. 'Art' as defined by J. D. Sedding 'is human or 'tis nothing. Real life forms its substance as well as its garniture.'[17] It was because the nineteenth century had lost touch with what the reformers conceived as 'reality' that its artefacts and its art industry were considered so pretentious, and so totally lacking in that unity of thought, feeling and execution that stamped the creation of what Reginald Blomfield called 'the living ages of the arts'. The reformers evoked the spirit of the vernacular, as expressed in the 'English house' which 'needs sparkling fires, radiant ingle-nooks, cheerful company, good fare, merry children, bright flowers, open windows, and vistas of well-polished furniture, mirrors, delft plates, and rows of shining pewter dishes, jugs, tankards, and braziers, to make it seem joyous'.[18] The extinction of the vernacular was evident in most industries, but it seemed painfully apparent in the debasement of furniture design—an emotive enough subject in any period and one to which the Arts and Crafts designers devoted a great deal of thought.

Furniture

In the *Arts and Crafts Essays*,[19] published in 1893, no fewer than eight of the contributions are concerned with the design and decoration of furniture, and the critics included Lethaby, Blomfield, Prior, Ricardo, J. H. Pollen and Stephen Webb, all of whom had worked in some capacity as furniture designers. Their standards had, of course, been set by William Morris, who, as we have seen, had distinguished between 'state' and 'cottage' furniture, and had approved of both where they were an expression of total architecture and the craftsman's joy in the execution of his work. His successors did not challenge this distinction, but they realized that the function of the so-called 'state' furniture might be misinterpreted in an age so devoted to the whims of fashion, and that its promotion might encourage the crime of 'cleverness'. For decoration, to be valid, must spring from a living tradition, and herein lay the failure of English display.

'Contrast, for instance [wrote Reginald Blomfield] a piece of Tottenham Court Rd marquetry with the mother-of-pearl and ebony inlay on an English cabinet at South Kensington. So far as mere skill in cutting goes, there may be no great difference between the two, but the latter is charming, and the former tedious in the last degree; and the reason is that in the seventeenth century the craftsman loved his work, and was master of it. He started with an idea in his head, and used his material with meaning, and so his inlay is as fanciful as the seaweed, and yet entirely subordinated to the whole design.' [20]

There were, of course, craftsmen such as Gimson and Voysey who worked with equal confidence in both 'styles' and their cabinets, like those of Ashbee and Baillie Scott, with their careful proportions and elaborate inlays were a demonstration of all Blomfield's criteria for good design. But although they were a perfect reflection of one aspect of what the Arts and Crafts required of furniture, the pieces were, even in their own time, anachronisms. It was their designers' so-called 'cottage' furniture, with its understatement, its straightforward construction, its sympathetic use of native woods and above all its sophistication, that pointed to one direction which furniture design was to take in the twentieth century. For this type of furniture, although craftsman-made, has an equivalent in quantity production, as the Scandinavians were to demonstrate, and as Thonet, at the time, was demonstrating. At the end of the nineteenth century Britain had, in its designers, the talent, and in its factories, the potential to emulate the Austrian and anticipate the Scandinavian achievement, but this was one of the few areas in which no attempt at a *rapprochement* was made; the gulf between the craft ideal and the product of the factory was never bridged, and it was left to such individuals as Ambrose Heal and Gordon Russell, and to a war-time utility scheme, to promote the ideal of sound, simple, unpretentious furniture for a mass market. At a time when the chair, as Crane put it, got 'more contemplation and attention than the palace' [21] the British designers felt they could not afford to compromise. Their ideas were menaced by factory shoddy, by the contrivances of the 'artistic furnisher' and by the fashion for antiques, and in these circumstances, they felt, they had only their own values, and their individualism to fall back on. Edward Prior, for example, in his contribution to the *Arts and Crafts Essays* called for designs that would express 'the heart of the age', but he anticipated the doctrinal differences that were to accompany the formation of the *Deutscher Werkbund* when he pleaded for individuality, rather than standardization in design. 'On the side of utility', he wrote, 'our furniture has been shaped to the uses of the million, not of the individual. Hence its monotonously average character, its failure to become part of ourselves, its lack of personal and local charm.' The converted, therefore, were urged to 'fight a good fight with commercialism', and to buy their furniture from 'the individual craftsman and not the commercial firm'.[22]

The cult of individualism, rather than commercialism, was to be responsible for the Art Nouveau demonstration of furniture as sculpture, but British designers, as we have seen, could not approve of such licence, and a gift of Art Nouveau furniture to the Victoria and Albert Museum in 1900 prompted an angry letter to *The Times*, signed, among others, by Reginald Blomfield. 'This work', they wrote, 'is neither right in principle nor does it evince a proper regard for the materials employed. As cabinet-makers' work it is badly executed. It represents only a trick of design which developed from debased forms, has prejudicially affected the design of furniture and buildings in neighbouring countries.'[23]

For furniture, according to Arts and Crafts principles, must be judged according to functional as well as aesthetic criteria; it must be well made, and above all it must be *convenient*. Criticism, therefore, both in the *Arts and Crafts Essays* and in journals such as the *Studio* anticipates the preoccupations of the twentieth-century consumer movements. Halsey Ricardo, for example, suffered from a storage problem:

'Take the common male chest of drawers as a case in point. Its function is to hold a man's shirts and his clothes, articles of a known and constant size. Why are the drawers not made proportionate for their duty? Why are they so few and so deep that when filled—as they needs must be—they are uneasy to draw out . . . It can hardly be economy of labour and material that dictates this, for—if so—why is the usual hanging wardrobe made so preposterously too tall?'[24]

The Studio, also, was consumer conscious, and the Yearbook of 1906, as well as evoking the general rule that decoration and ornament should be subordinate to structure, also states that 'surfaces where dust and dirt can accumulate and not easily be removed are to be avoided as far as possible'; chests of drawers, for example, must not be so low on the ground that the housemaid cannot sweep under them, nor should wardrobe tops be too high.

Apart from the work of the Century Guild and Morris & Company the first attempt to launch a furniture firm on Arts and Crafts principles came in 1890 when a group of young architects, Lethaby, Gimson, Mervyn Macartney, Sidney Barnsley and Reginald Blomfield, set up Kenton & Co. (A fifth, non-designing member of the firm, was a Colonel Mallet 'who had taste and knew people'.) 'We set out', wrote Blomfield, 'to make the best possible furniture of its time, with the best materials and the best workmanship attainable, and as we hoped, the best designs, for we made the designs ourselves, bought our own materials and supervised our own workmen in our shops.'[25] For two years the group achieved a modest success. They held an exhibition in

Barnard's Inn in 1891 and sold £700-worth of furniture, but lack of capital hampered progress, and the enterprise folded in 1892.

Lethaby, Macartney and Blomfield had provided the inspiration for this enterprise, but it was the younger members, Ernest Gimson and the two Barnsley brothers, who decided to specialize in furniture design, and who retired to a rural retreat in order to devote themselves to their crafts. Gimson came from Leicester and the Barnsleys, Sidney and Ernest, from Birmingham. All three had arrived in London in 1886—Gimson on Morris's recommendation to work in J. D. Sedding's office, where Ernest Barnsley was also an apprentice, while Sidney joined Lethaby and Norman Shaw. Before he came to London, Gimson's 'elected prophets' according to Lethaby were 'Ruskin, Morris, Auberon Herbert and Herbert Spencer'.[26] He and Lethaby were immediately sympathetic; they spent their weekends rambling in the countryside, and after long discussions defined architecture as 'building touched with emotion', and art as 'doing not designing': 'work not words, things not designs, life not rewards were his aims', declared Lethaby in his characteristic style.

Gimson had been apprenticed to a local architect in Leicester and had also studied at the Leicester School of Art before he came to London; during the London period he joined the Society for the Protection of Ancient Buildings, and inspired by lectures at the Art-Workers' Guild, decided to master certain crafts that were in danger of extinction. He studied plaster work with Whitcombe and Priestley in London, and he spent a fortnight at Bosbury in Herefordshire, where Philip Clissett, a chair bodger, taught him how to make the traditional rush-seated designs in turned ash. He left London with the Barnsleys in 1893, moving first to Ewen, near Cirencester, then to Pinbury, where they set up workshops, and finally to Sapperton, where the Daneway workshops were established in 1902; Gimson remained there until his death in 1919.

Gimson had built a house for himself in Leicester in 1892, but he never lived in it and it was not until 1897 that he began to build his few houses and cottages inspired by the ideal of the hamlet. Here, for example, is his description of the building of Long Orchard at Budleigh Salterton in 1911, whose walls were of cob and whose timbers were of English chestnut. 'The cob', says Gimson, 'was made of stiff sand found on the site; this was mixed with water and a great quantity of long wheat straw trodden in it. The walls were built 3 ft thick, pared down to 2 ft 6 ins, . . . and built of cobble stones found among the sand. The walls were given a coat of plaster and a coat of rough cast, which was gently trowelled over to smooth the surface slightly.'[27] Gimson's interiors were conceived in the same spirit; the cottage at Pinbury, which he converted, and in which he lived for ten years had stone-flagged floors, and the walls, ceilings, beams and joists were white; 'a large black dresser hung with gay and well used crockery, a large settle at the fireside and an oak arm-chair and other rush bottom chairs, made by himself, were its furniture'.[28]

Gimson, in fact, made very little of his own furniture and while Sidney Barnsley, a total purist, made all his own designs, Gimson's were executed by his craftsmen according to the precedent established by Kenton & Co. His aim was to produce work that was 'useful and right, pleasantly shaped and finished, good enough, but not too good for ordinary use'.[29] Native woods were generally used, oak, elm, yew and walnut, and again according to Lethaby 'every piece was thought definitely for particular woods and for clearly understood ways of workmanship, and the supervision was so constant and so thorough that the design was changed in the process of making as the materials and working might suggest'. As well as his deceptively simple cottage designs, Gimson also produced 'prestige' pieces inlaid with mother of pearl, silver, ivory and bone, a practice which was no doubt encouraged by Peter van der Waals, the Dutch cabinet-maker who joined the group in 1901, and who in 1935 became design adviser to Loughborough Training College in an attempt to improve design education in the schools.[30]

Gimson's furniture is now considered part of the English tradition, and Pevsner has defined him, with justice, as 'the greatest English artist-craftsman'.[31] Its value, however, was not immediately apparent to his contemporaries, and while the *Studio* was always unstinting in its praise of his work other critics were less appreciative; a correspondent in *Country Life* felt that his furniture had 'too close a kinship with the packing case'[32] while *The Builder* complained that 'the new school of furniture designers appears to be losing the sense of style and of the dignity of design which accompanies it altogether. The object now seems to be to make a thing as square, as plain, as devoid of any beauty of line as is possible and to call this art.'[33]

The analogy with twentieth-century preoccupations is obvious, although the motivation was so different. It is interesting to note, however, that although Gimson could never conceive of working in any other way, and although he complained to Lethaby about the ideals of the Design and Industries Association,[34] he could not totally condemn machine work; Alfred Powell, the potter who was associated with the Cotswold group, attributes this prophetic remark to Gimson: 'Let machinery be honest and make its own machine buildings and its own machine furniture; let it make its chairs of stamped aluminium if it likes: why not?'[35]

Glass and textiles

Ideas such as these tended by this time to be assumptions in the United States, and in Europe they were to form the basis of a new machine aesthetic; they were not, in fact, completely alien to British thinking, although to the majority of theorists manufacturers were only considered 'progressive' where they had absorbed the message of the crafts. Writing about 'Table Glass', for example, in the *Arts and Crafts Essays*, Somers Clarke was able to report that 'the old decanter, a massive lump of misshapen material better suited to the purpose of braining a burglar than decorating a table, has given place to a light and gracefully formed vessel, covered in many cases with well-designed surface engraving, and thoroughly suited both to the uses it is intended to fulfil and the material of which it is made',[36] while Walter Crane conceded that as far as wallpaper production was concerned 'very remarkable results have been produced, and a special development of applied design may almost be said to have come into existence with the modern use of wallpapers'.[37]

It is significant that in both the glass and wallpaper industries, individual manu-facturers were sympathetic to the Arts and Crafts cause; James Powell & Sons, for example, had produced the stained glass used by Morris and his colleagues, and in response to Ruskin's comments on the nature of glass in the *Stones of Venice*, had begun to introduce simple, uncut ranges of table glass. Philip Webb had designed such a set for use in the Red House (see pl 14) and later in the century the production of similar ranges was further encouraged by Harry J. Powell, who anticipated the Orrefors revolution by designing and marketing ranges that relied on qualities of form, rather than decoration, for their appeal. Nor is it surprising that the design profession in England found enthusiastic supporters in the textile and wallpaper industries; there was little difficulty here in relating the aesthetic to either craft or machine production and, furthermore, it was to the manufacturer's advantage to seek advice in matters of taste, and so challenge the supremacy of the French. Metford Warner, of Jeffrey & Co, played a pioneering rôle here. He had joined the firm as a junior partner in 1866 and had taken charge in 1871, establishing the firm's tradition of collaboration with freelance designers. As well as working with Morris, he pro-duced wallpapers designed by Owen Jones, Bruce Talbert, William Burges, Crane and Godwin, and by 1878 the firm's prestige was such that the *Art Journal* was able to state that its work 'not only rivalled, but surpassed the produce of Paris that for so long monopolised the market'.[38] Similar transformations were taking place in textile design, so that by the 1880s and '90s British achievements were provoking those Continental cries of delight described by Samuel Bing. Nevertheless such sophistica-tion, however well justified and demonstrated by Morris and his contemporaries, was a far cry from the ideal of the homespun, as defined by Ruskin, and hand-weaving, like craft pottery, is an essentially twentieth-century phenomenon. However, some of the impetus for the revival of hand-weaving and its subsequent influence on woven fabrics could be said to have been supplied by Ruskin. In the 1870s, for example, he took up the cause of the hand-spinners in the Isle of Man, acquiring a water mill for them and encouraging them to produce wool cloth of high quality, guaranteed to 'last forever'. In 1883, when Ruskin's health was failing, he handed over the enterprise to a Huddersfield manufacturer, George Thomson, who inspired by Ruskin's teaching was running his woollen mill on co-operative lines.[39] Towards the end of his life Ruskin also did a great deal to revive cottage industries in Westmorland and Cumber-land: Albert Fleming, for example, who established the Langdale Weaving Industry in 1883, did so on Ruskin's encouragement, and this was followed by Annie Garnett's Windermere Spinnery in 1891. Handloom weaving workshops were also set up in Haslemere in the 1890s, and Katie Grasett's famous London School of Weaving, which survived until very recently, was first established in 1898. Enterprises such as these were further encouraged by the Home Arts and Industries Association, estab-lished in 1884, the same year as the Art-Worker's Guild, and dedicated to teaching home employments, such as 'spinning and knitting, sewing and tailoring, carpentry and cabinet-making, basket work and boat-building'.[40] Its Scottish branch, for example, did a great deal to revive the Highland Home Industries, while in 1887 the

158

government gave a grant of £1000 so that teachers could be trained to further the ideals of the Donegal Industrial Fund, which sold the products of village industries. 'Slowly and laboriously we are working on', reported Mrs Ernest Hart, the original sponsor of the scheme, 'and in a land where there were no arts, where despair and poverty reigned, a better day is dawning, and we look forward to the time, not we trust far distant, when in the hand loom, the tambour frame, and carpenter's shop, and the dye vat, the Irish peasant who chooses to live on the shores of the wild Atlantic, and who still preserves the to us lost treasure of leisure, may produce beautiful and original work.'[41]

Silver and metalwork

The Arts and Crafts movement produced several distinguished silversmiths, who, unlike the textile, wallpaper and pottery designers, received little or no support from what they despairingly called 'the trade'. In the last decades of the nineteenth century production in this field had become totally debased; Christopher Dresser, whose work and genius were unique, was one of the few designers producing original work for industry, and W. A. S. Benson, in his lecture on *Metal Work* for the Arts and Crafts Exhibition Society, accurately described the commercial approach:

'Unhappily there is little original English work being done in these metals. The more ordinary wares have all life and feeling taken out of them by mechanical finish, an abrasive process being employed to remove every sign of tool marks. The all important surface is thus obliterated. As to design, fashion oscillates between copies of one past period and another. A comparison between copies of one of these copies with an original will make the distinction between the work of a man paid to do his quickest, and one paid to do his best, clearer than volumes of description.'

Benson was one of several metal-workers who set up their own workshops in the 1880s and 1890s, and although he rarely attempted to formulate his ideas in writing,[42] he had already by the turn of the century begun to translate the Arts and Crafts philosophy into ideals for industrial production. He was a founder member of the Art-Workers' Guild and, significantly, some thirty years later, he was one of the original members of the Design and Industries Association. He was born in 1854, and his mother, according to W. H. Bruce, in the preface to Benson's book *Drawing—its history and its uses*,[43] was 'an ardent student of Ruskin'. The young Benson, however, whose uncle had introduced him to 'the mysteries and delights of elementary mechanics', aspired to be an engineer. His education (Winchester and New College, Oxford) did little to encourage such pursuits, and in 1878 he was articled to Basil Champneys, the architect, sharing lodgings with Heywood Sumner who married his sister. It was at this time that he first got to know Burne-Jones and Morris, and with the latter's encouragement opened a small workshop for the production of metalwork in 1880. His father provided financial help in the early stages, and in 1882 he moved into larger premises, establishing a foundry in an old malt house in Chiswick Mall;

this venture obviously met with some success, since shortly afterwards he built a factory in Hammersmith, and in 1887 opened his showrooms in Bond Street.

Benson, a realistic and eminently practical designer, followed contemporary commercial machine techniques in his workshops, and produced inexpensive domestic ware (see pl 70). (This no doubt accounts for his staying power, for the firm continued production until 1920, when Benson retired.) As well as hollow-ware, he designed lampshades and electric lighting fittings and the *Studio* Yearbook in 1906 praises the experiments he had carried out with reflectors, which, as the article points out, meet a 'self-evident proposition [that] the primary function of all lighting apparatus is to give light', an 'essential not by any means invariably fulfilled'. After the death of Morris, Benson, who had also designed furniture, became a director of Morris & Co, and together with Mervyn Macartney and George Jack, designed several cabinets for the Firm. Benson, however, was unique among Arts and Crafts practitioners in that, as his obituary in *The Times* pointed out,[44] he 'preferred to approach his subject as an engineer rather than a hand-worker; to produce his beautiful forms by machinery on a commercial scale rather than single works of art'. Admittedly, in order to do this to his own satisfaction he had to set up his own factory, but having done this he demonstrated that machine work could be as viable as the hand product if the potential of the material and production methods were properly understood. His obituary aptly described his attitude to his work:

'His lamps, vases, entrée dishes, etc., were all the outcome of profound study of the capabilities of heavy stamping plant, spinning lathes and shaping tools which he was able to put down in his Hammersmith works . . . Visitors to the works who knew him as a rather dreary artist . . . were amazed and almost aghast to find themselves in what appeared to be an engineering workshop full of large machines . . . and a lacquering department which had benefitted so much from his inventive genius that constant efforts were made by trade rivals to penetrate its secrets.'

Several other 'self-taught' metal-workers established their own studios in the 1880s and 1890s; they worked on a smaller scale, and many of them became teachers when the Schools of Art began to appoint practising designers to their staff. Henry Wilson, Alexander Fisher, Llewellyn Rathbone and George Frampton, for example, were all associated with the London Central School. It was in Birmingham, Pugin's 'inexhaustible mine of bad taste', that the first positive steps were taken to offer training that would be directly related to the city's industries. The Birmingham School of Design, established in 1843, had its own metalwork department, and in the 1890s was directed by Edward R. Taylor, a progressive headmaster, who fired his students with an enthusiasm for the ideals of William Morris. Moreover, in 1890 the city council, recognizing the need for more specialized training, had established a new branch school for jewellers and silversmiths at Vittoria Street under the direction of R. Catterson-Smith. During the '90s Birmingham, mainly through the impetus of its art school, became a flourishing centre for guild-inspired activities. Staff and students from the school formed the Birmingham Group of Painters and Craftsmen and a

Guild of Handicraft was founded there in 1895 by Arthur Dixon (pls 72 and 73) a silversmith trained as an architect, who was a friend both of Morris and Ashbee. Arthur Gaskin (pl 75), a painter, metal-worker and illustrator, who was trained and taught at the School of Art, was appointed headmaster of the Vittoria Street School in 1902, and John Cooper, who had been articled to J. D. Sedding and Henry Wilson, became head of the metalwork department in 1904. Instruction, both in the College of Art and its branch schools was intended to be directly related to the needs of the city's industries; local elementary schools released their pupils so that they could be taught there for part of the week from the ages of twelve to fourteen, and 'remedial' courses were also offered for older workmen.

Between 1900 and 1914 most British art schools were reorganized along similar lines, with staff drawn from the ranks of the Art-Workers' Guild, and during this period, which culminated in the formation of the Design and Industries Association, a valiant attempt was made to relate the craft ideal to the needs of industry. It was inevitable that the impetus for such a *rapprochement* should come from within the Arts and Crafts movement, for just as social commitment had forced Morris to consider the wider implications of his preoccupations and to readjust his attitudes to machine production, in the same way a number of his successors also began to realize that the product, as well as the potential of the machine, could not be ignored, and that the craft ideal, if it were to have any significance on either a social or aesthetic level must be reinterpreted to serve the needs of industrial rather than individual endeavour. Ironically, ideas such as these, which had first been tentatively formulated by the reformers of the 1840s and '50s, and which had been discredited by Ruskinian ideal- ism, re-emerged during the 1880s and '90s just at the time when the Arts and Crafts movement was 'officially' launched with the formation of the Art-Workers' Guild, the Arts and Crafts Exhibition Society and the Home Arts and Industries Association.

National Association for the Advancement of Art and its Application to Industry

Of the various societies that were established in England in the 1880s the National Association for the Advancement of Art and its Application to Industry is the least well known, but its aims and ideology were as pertinent to contemporary and future theory as were those of the Art-Workers' Guild and the Arts and Crafts societies. Its initial inspiration was no doubt the French *Union Centrale des Beaux-Arts appliqués à l'Industrie*, with its motto *Le Beau dans l'Utile*, which had been established in 1863 as part of that general movement towards design reform, which resulted from the Great Exhibition; but whereas the *Union Centrale* was the rallying point for that unique French phenomenon, the *artiste décorateur*, its British equivalent, predictably enough, was a more sober affair, seeking by means of congresses held in the major manufacturing cities to promote the ideals of art in industry, and to quote Mack- murdo who was very much involved in the negotiations, to give the manufacturer 'some better understanding of the relation of industry to life'.[45]

The National Association was set up in 1887, and its first Congress was held in Liverpool in 1888. The list of officers on this occasion makes impressive reading; the President was Sir Frederick Leighton, and the Vice-Presidents included the Earl of Derby, the Earl of Pembroke and the Earl of Wharncliffe, as well as Sir John Everett Millais, Bart, RA, while Edmund Gosse, Philip Rathbone, George Howard, Mackmurdo and Cosmo Monkhouse were on the central committee and in charge of various sections. (As Honorary Secretary to the association, Mackmurdo was able to persuade Morris, who had given an address on *Art and its Producers* to the Liverpool Congress in 1888, to act as president of the Applied Art Section in Edinburgh the next year, although, according to Mackmurdo, Morris 'doubted the wisdom of speaking his mind' at such gatherings.) Three congresses were held in all, the first in Liverpool, the second in Edinburgh and the third in Birmingham; during these three sessions audiences heard talks by architects, industrialists and educationists, as well as by leading members of the crafts lobby, and speakers included Whistler, Madox Brown, Voysey, Sedding, Lewis Day and Patrick Geddes. 'It was a fairly representative parliament' wrote Walter Crane. 'The royal academician sat down with the socialist; the scientific colour theorist fed with the practical decorator; the industrial villager faced the manufacturer; the art critic and the painter mingled their tears, and all were led to the pasture by a gentle Fine Art professor.'[46]

Reading these transactions today, however, and comparing them with the attitudes expressed in the *Arts and Crafts Essays*, one is struck by the radicalism, the prescience and the sound common sense of many of the proposals. In spite of the existence, on the one hand, of a seemingly flourishing art industry, and on the other of a healthy renaissance of craft ideals, it was obvious to many of the speakers that Britain's success was based on the flimsiest of foundations, and that sound conditions, both for the advancement of art and its application to industry, were virtually non-existent. The British sickness was diagnosed and analysed, and as many cures as there were speakers were recommended. It was apparent, however, perhaps because of the very nature of the enterprise they represented, that many of the speakers could no longer accept the Ruskinian attitudes to art and industry, and their statements defining the values of industrial production have a prophetic, or to some ears at least, a disturbingly twentieth-century ring.

A recurrent theme, and one that was to be expected, was the failure of the art schools. 'After some thirty years of enormous expenditure to popularise art', complained J. E. Hodgson, RA, 'our manufacturers are just where they were . . . instead of the artist educating the manufacturer, it is the manufacturer who has to educate the artist.'[47] Several speakers insisted that matters were better organized in other countries, and as in 1835 the German approach to such problems was recommended. One speaker, A. Harris, had recently visited Germany, touring the design schools, and although he detected and deplored a passion for 'florid and rococo ornamentation' he felt that these schools, in that they encouraged a healthy liaison between designer, manufacturer and consumer, were far more successful and more practical than their British counterparts, and that although British best was superior to German best, it was too élitist to have any practical influence on general standards. His comparison between work shown at the Arts and Crafts Exhibition Society's display in London and an exhibition of industrial art in Munich served to demonstrate this point, for 'whereas in England the productions are those of an aesthetic community of very limited extent and influence, Munich affords a complete compendium of modern German art, and whilst in Munich the traders, designers and handicraftsmen of every class are abundantly represented, in England the general trader and the working craftsmen are conspicuous chiefly by their absence'.

Remarks such as these, which implied the possibility of compromise on aesthetic standards in order to achieve commercial viability, must have seemed abrasive enough within an Arts and Crafts context, but other speakers were to be far more iconoclastic. R. Rowand Anderson, for example, president of the architectural section at Edinburgh in 1889, opened the session with an attack on Ruskinian ethics and aesthetics. Quoting the first axiom of *Seven Lamps* he insisted that 'such doctrines . . . are contradicted by everything we see in nature, and all we can learn from Grecian and mediaeval art. Art is not applied to any object in nature; the beauty we see there, and what seems by contrast the ugliness in the lower animals and plants, is inseparable from their structure and its functions which fit them for their environment and the purposes for which they have been created.' [48] He then goes on to express attitudes to functionalism which recall the by then seemingly discredited preoccupations of Semper, Digby Wyatt and their colleagues in the 1850s and which anticipate the pronouncements of Wagner, Van de Velde, Corbusier, Loos, Frank Lloyd Wright and the Futurists:

'Who has looked down into the engine room of one of the great ocean steamers and not felt the impression of an irresistible power that rests not day nor night. Look at a shearing or punching machine, that opens and closes its jaws, and cuts or punches iron plates, just as easily as cutting paper; the steam hammer, planing machine and pumping machines all have the same clear expression of their purpose . . . The designing of machinery, whether for peace or war, has now reached such a high standard of excellence in function, form and expression that one is justified in saying that these things are entitled to rank as works of art as much as a painting, a piece of sculpture, or a building, and also that machinery is the only true constructive art that has been produced since the decline of mediaeval architecture.'

These are fighting words, and they are remarkable for their futuristic quality. Difficult as it is to believe that they were spoken at a British design congress in the 1880s, they were, nevertheless, indicative of a very positive shift in attitudes, for other theorists were at the same time exploring the necessity for a machine, as opposed to craft, aesthetic. In 1882, for example, Lewis Day, writing about *Everyday Art*, had insisted that 'machinery and steam power, and electricity for all we know will have something to say concerning the ornament of the future',[49] a theme that was to be re-examined by John Sedding at the Liverpool Congress in 1888.

John Sedding was the brother of Edmund, who was working in Street's office when

Morris joined them, and he too had worked for Street in the early 1860s, along with Norman Shaw. According to Lethaby he 'drew tenderly in a Ruskinian way' and 'saw as few of his time had seen that architecture was workmanship rather than paper, and that spirit came before forms'.[50] He set up his own architectural practice in London in 1874 in offices next door to the headquarters of Morris & Co, and as well as designing embroidery, wallpapers and ecclesiastical ware, his work included St Peter's Church, Ealing, and Holy Trinity, Sloane Street. Sedding gathered round him a distinguished circle of associates. Henry Wilson was his chief assistant, Barnsley and Gimson both worked for him, and he gave Christopher Whall, the glass painter, his first commission, to design the east window of the Lady Chapel of St Mary's, Stamford. He was appointed master of the Art-Workers' Guild in 1886 in succession to Walter Crane, and he published *Art and Handicraft*, a collection of his lectures and papers, in 1893.[51] He belongs, therefore, to the main tradition of the Arts and Crafts movement, and William Morris is his lodestar. His conception of Morris, however, is somewhat different from that of his contemporaries: 'Fancy what a year of grace it were for England, if our industries were placed under the guidance of "one vast Morris". Fancy a Morris installed in every factory—the Joseph of every grinding Pharaoh. The battle of the industries were half won!' The quotation is taken from his speech to the Liverpool Congress in 1888, in which he identified Morris, who had his own workshops, 'put an apron on, tucked up his sleeves, and set to work' with the cause of industrial rather than craft design.

Sedding's opinions, therefore, represent a shift in attitude that is no less significant than that of Dr Anderson; for although he is never as radical as the latter, his nostalgia relates, not to the mediaeval past but to the early days of the Industrial Revolution, when, he maintains, the manufacturer shared the life of his workmen and did not 'fly the poisoned air and the blackened fields and streams as he does now'. He built mills and factories that were 'neither beautiful nor hideous, but just plain and suited to their purpose', and before the 'paper designers' came on to the scene, the 'old hands' were satisfactorily adapting the traditional values and standards to the new techniques of manufacture. Like Morris, Sedding insists that it is not the machines that are at fault but the men who direct them; he is more emphatic than Morris, however, in stressing that future programmes of reform must be directed towards factory production, and that any system that ignores this basic fact was doomed to failure. 'Let us not suppose', he said, 'that machinery will be discontinued. Manufacture cannot be organised on any other basis. We had better recognise this, better make life square with the facts, rather than rebel against the actual and inevitable, in striving for the ideal.' He then went on to elaborate a craft/machine aesthetic which comes close to the theories that the German *Werkbund* and the Design and Industries Association were to elaborate some twenty years later:[52]

'Our manufactures must be of good material and make. The designs must be good and well suited to the necessities of modern methods of production. Note, moreover, that it is not good enough to get good designs, but the designer should, more or less, supplement their making at the factory. The designer should be part of the working staff of the factory, see his design take shape, and be consulted as required. We have had enough of mere studio designs. And as to technical schools, however admirable in their way, the instruction they can give is not perfect. The best school for art-industry is a wholesome factory. And the ideal factory is a place where the artist-designer is a handicraftsman and the handicraftsman is an artist in his way.'[52]

With Sedding, therefore, the twentieth-century design aesthetic is beginning to emerge, and his vision of the ideal factory was to a certain extent to be realized in Scandinavia where the creative artist and designer has a positive role to play in factory production. In England the situation was, in theory, an ideal one; there was no dearth of creative talent, and there was, within certain sectors of industry, an intelligent desire to support and exploit that talent. But for British designers the realization that the ideals they had formulated could and should be related to the field of industrial production came too late, and since it came to each designer more or less as a personal revelation, there was no attempt to formulate a corporate theory until the establishment of the Design and Industries Association in 1914. The efforts of the National Association represented a positive *rapprochement* between the craft lobby and the promoters of art in industry, but opinion was too confused for any firm policy line to develop, and no strong individual figure emerged to define and promote the new cause.

The two men who were to establish themselves as major design theorists at the turn of the century were C. R. Ashbee and W. R. Lethaby, but it was not until the years immediately preceding the first world war that they began to question the assumptions of Morris and Ruskin, and recognize that production by machinery was not necessarily wholly evil. Lethaby, as an educator, probably exerted a wider influence, but Ashbee's experience is interesting in that he, of all Ruskin's followers, made the most vigorous and sustained attempt to establish a rural 'workshop paradise', and having experienced the failure of all his early ideals went on to formulate a practical policy for design reform that was, in some measure, relevant to the realities of the first decades of the twentieth century.

6 Ashbee and the craft of the machine

'Old Morris was delightful, firing up with the warmth of his subject . . . At length, banging his hand upon the table: "No!" said he. "The thing is this; if we had our Revolution tomorrow, what should we socialists do the day after?" "Yes—what?" we all cried. And that he could not answer. "We should all be hanged, because we are promising the people more than we can ever give them." '[1]

The reminiscences are those of Charles Robert Ashbee, a recent recruit to the cause of architecture, socialism and the crafts. He had gone to hear his friend Edward Carpenter speak to the Hammersmith Branch of the Socialist League; the meeting was held in Morris's house and Ashbee was full of enthusiasm for the ideas and idealism of his new colleagues. He had just emerged from a conventional upper-middle-class education at Wellington and King's College, Cambridge, where he had read history, and was training, under G. F. Bodley, the first patron of the Firm, to be an architect.

Of all the designers working within the Arts and Crafts movement, Ashbee probably gained the keenest knowledge of the realities of life for the working man, for he spent the first fifteen years of his career as a designer in the East End, establishing the Essex House Press, as well as the Guild and School of Handicraft there. Ashbee's association with the East End began in 1886 when he was first articled to Bodley. At that time he was living at Toynbee Hall, the pioneer university settlement which had just been founded by Canon Samuel Barnett; Ashbee had no doubt been introduced to the settlement by Edward Carpenter, who had joined the staff of the University Extension Movement when it was founded in 1874. Carpenter was a friend both of Morris and the Socialist Hyndman, and had visited the States in 1877, when he had met Whitman; he undoubtedly made a profound impression on the young Ashbee, who felt that 'the teachings of Edward Carpenter, and the writings of Walt Whitman were a healthy counterblast to the profession, to ecclesiasticism, and above all to the unrealities of Toynbee Hall'.[2]

For Toynbee Hall, in spite of its good intentions, was a disappointment to him; it had, he wrote, 'no corporate life; it was neither a college, convent nor a club'[3] and he was to compare it unfavourably with Hull House,* which was directly inspired by

* Hull House was founded in 1889 by Jane Addams, and during the 1880s and '90s many Americans visited the British settlement in order to study its aims and methods. Some insight into the activities that they might have observed there is provided by Charles Booth, also associated with Toynbee Hall, who began his investigations into the *Life and Labour of the People* in 1886; in Volume

the London settlement. Ashbee was the only architect in residence when he joined the settlement; his contribution was to start a Ruskin reading class, and, encouraged by its success, he also began to teach drawing and decoration. Members of this class decorated the Toynbee Hall dining-room, and they were to form the nucleus of his Guild of Handicraft, which he founded in 1888 with three members, and a working capital of £50. Despite the obvious economic difficulties the Guild flourished and expanded; in 1890 Ashbee took over the lease of Essex House 'a stately Georgian mansion in Mile End', at the same time opening retail premises at 16a Brook Street, and in 1898 he founded the Essex House Press, buying two of the Albion presses Morris had used, and employing several of the Kelmscott craftsmen.

During the early years Ashbee and his guildsmen were self-taught, acquiring their skills by trial and error; this, according to Ashbee, was the only way a craft could be mastered, an individualistic style emerging from team work and shared experience. In *Modern English Silverwork*, issued by the Essex House Press in 1909, he describes how 'style and character' are formed by the acquisition of technical skills, allied to a knowledge of past achievements:

'It is in the learning how to do things and do them well, that many fresh design motives are evolved. So it comes that when a little group of men learn to pull together in a workshop, to trust each other, to play into each other's hand, and understand each other's limitations, their combination becomes creative, and the character that they develop in themselves takes expression in the work of their fingers. Humanity and craftsmanship are essential.'[4]

Ashbee shared the traditional Arts and Crafts distrust of the 'trade' and of the design schools; as far as he was concerned art school and trade workshop experience were 'a positive disadvantage', and he described the designing class in the School of Handicraft, which he ran in conjunction with the Guild until 1895, as

'. . . the backbone of the school. Each pupil is taught first to conceive the design, and then to apply it through the help of the other classes to the different materials, the wood, the metal, the clay, the gesso, the flat surface for painting. The effort here, therefore, is not to emulate the ordinary Technical School but to follow in the lines laid down by leading artists who have the encouragement of the handicrafts at heart, in the belief that the modern cry for the education of the hand and eye can only be fully achieved in the education of the individuality of the workman.'[5]

---

1 Booth describes the aims of the settlement and one week's 'bill of fare'. This included lectures on *Socrates*, *The Chemistry of Arts and Manufacturers*, *Starfish* and *The Physiology of the Senses*; there were classes in Latin, Greek and French as well as in carpentry, decoration, wood-carving, clay-modelling and Venetian art; reading parties in Plato, Bacon and Spinoza were also underway. 'Something of this kind', according to Booth, 'goes on every week. There are over 600 members on the register of the classes, and 600 tickets were sold for the last course of University Extension lectures. In all about 1,000 people come weekly to Toynbee Hall for concerts, lectures, classes, etc.' (Vol 1, first edition, 1889).

The original members of the Guild were John Pearson, John Williams, W. A. White and William Hardiman; in his unpublished *Memoirs* Ashbee described how he first came across White at Toynbee Hall, working as an assistant in a City bookshop, and Hardiman's origins seem equally romantic. 'He was one of the finest modellers I ever came across,' wrote Ashbee, 'his touch was exquisite. I made his acquaintance first in 1888 in Whitechapel, where he was earning 15s a week by trundling a catsmeat barrow. He came to the School of Handicraft in the evenings, and I was struck with the extraordinary fidelity and feeling with which he made a copy of the St Cecilia of Donatello.'[6]

Pearson, the first metalwork instructor, is more of an enigma, and he may have worked for William De Morgan as a potter before he joined the Guild.[7] Shirley Bury has also suggested[8] that he may have learned the craft through the Home Arts and Industries Association, or taught himself by using one of Charles Leland's * teaching manuals.

Once its teething troubles were over, however, the Guild and its workmen succeeded in establishing a distinctive style in design and execution. Ashbee lists 'pianos, bedsteads, wallpapers, clocks, cast-iron ware and pottery' among the products he designed for industry;[9] metalwork, silverware and furniture, however, formed the major part of the Guild's production, and the Guild Roll from 1887 to 1908[10] includes nineteen cabinet-makers, fifteen metal-workers and silversmiths, nine jewellers, one enameller, one engraver, one chaser and two blacksmiths among its members. As with the majority of the Arts and Crafts designers, the stylistic influences on Ashbee's work are varied. He acknowledges his debt to Cellini in that the first production of his Press in 1898 was his own translation of the *Treatises*, and he uses simple robust forms that are reminiscent of mediaeval silverwork, often with the stylized naturalistic motifs that are characteristic of Art Nouveau. Ashbee, of course, would have considered any association of his work with Art Nouveau as an insult; in fact his contempt for the movement inspired him to verse:

> I'm in the fashion—non controversial,
> And the fashion is nothing if not commercial,
> Pre-Raphaelite once, with a tiny twist

---

* Charles G. Leland, an American, was living in England in the 1880s, and in a lecture to the Royal Society of Arts in 1885, he described how the impetus for his teaching had come from seeing Egyptian children designing and producing craftwork, and how, during his stay in England he published 'a small work on the minor arts, in which I suggested that classes for studying them might be formed in every village, or its school'. This, he claims, was the inspiration for Mrs Jebb and the work of the Home Arts and Industries Association; he also put his theories into practice in his native Philadelphia, where some 200 schoolchildren produced and sold craftwork. 'To help these classes, I published in America a series of 12 hand-books on such subjects as design, wood-carving, modelling, embroidery, stencilling, papier-mache, painting, leather-work.' Similar hand-books were available in England, and Mrs Bury cites a report in the *Star* in 1899 which pointed to the resemblance between the early work of the Guild and Leland's suggested designs for brass and copper.

Of the philosophical hedonist,
Inspired by Whistler—next a touch
Of the 'Arts and Crafts', but not too much.
Then Impressionism, the daintiest fluke;
Then the German squirm, and the Glasgow spook,
A spice of the latest French erotic,
Anything new and Studiotic,
As long as it tells in black and white,
And however wrong comes out all right,
'Id est', as long as it pays, you know,
That's what's meant by L'Art Nouveau![11]

Ashbee produced a wide range of silverware for private and ecclesiastical clients; each piece was individual and many were works of art in their own right. His designs included simple dishes and salvers, embellished by the hammer, as well as more elaborate pieces, incorporating wirework, semi-precious stones and enamel. There are inevitably hints of German squirm and Glasgow spook, but Ashbee's work, always delicate, controlled and understated, met with the approval of the discerning critic: 'Mr Ashbee', according to the *Studio*,[12] 'gains an effect of superb richness, in the right way. That is to say, he knows when to be silent, when to let the broad sweep of undecorated surface prepare you for the final ornamentation which heightens the beauty of the object, instead of hiding it under a superfluous mass of applied decoration.' (See pls 80–83.)

During the last decade of the nineteenth century Ashbee had achieved international as well as national fame. He exhibited in most of the Arts and Crafts Exhibition Society displays, and 'Magpie and Stump', the family house which he built in Cheyne Walk, London, in 1895, and which was decorated throughout by the Guild (pl 78), was discussed and illustrated in the *Studio* in 1895, and again in an article by Hermann Muthesius in *Dekorative Kunst* in 1898. In 1897 Ashbee writes to tell his fiancée that the Grand Duke of Hesse had sent a special envoy from Darmstadt to see his work,[13] and it was as a result of these enquiries that the architect, Baillie Scott, was commissioned to decorate the Grand Duke's Palace, the designs being carried out by the Guild (see pl 88). Then in 1899 Ashbee records that 'an interesting Hungarian has turned up'; the latter, being the Secretary of the Hungarian Economics Association, was 'in touch with most of the younger economists or such as have had anything to do with the teachings of John Ruskin and their practical bearing, and therefore gravitates like driftwood to Brook Street'.[14] The result was a commission 'to do all the furniture and fittings of his house, the silverwork, even to the book-plate of his library at Budapest and Pressburg with a possible new house to follow . . .'; Josef Hoffmann's Vienna Workshops were inspired by the Guild,[15] and in *An Endeavour toward the teaching of Ruskin and Morris* (1901) Ashbee described how for many years he had been involved in a 'continuous round of Exhibits to Manchester, Liverpool, Dublin, Berlin, Munich, Frankfurt, Paris and the Cape'.

The Guild of Handicraft at Chipping Campden

In 1902, however, when the Guild was flourishing and expanding, the lease on Essex House expired, and failing to find suitable alternative premises in London, Ashbee transferred his activities to Chipping Campden in Gloucestershire. This move to the country was no doubt idealistic rather than expedient, and it is interesting to note that Morris and De Morgan had, in fact, considered Campden before they took over the premises in Merton, but had felt that the village, although idyllic, was too far from London.[16] The decision to move the Guild was characteristically a democratic one, Ashbee conducting a poll among Guild members: 'The woodshop and smith are solid for going,' he wrote, 'the metalshop and Press are divided.'[17] In the end about fifty craftsmen and their families—some 150 people in all—descended on the village, their priorities being to convert and restore the dilapidated cottages, to re-establish their workshops and last but not least, to overcome local opposition and suspicion since the disruption to the pattern of village life, with its traditional hierarchies, was obviously resented.

'The sort of opposition a London community had in the countryside in those days is inconceivable now. When Shakespeare's *As you like it* was given in the Town Hall the managers of the Church Schools, led by the parson, tried to prevent the children from attending the performance. As for the farmers, they put their representatives on the Technical School Committee established by the Board of Education. They did this not because they wanted to hurt the Guild or its enterprise, but because they considered that anything in the nature of educating the labourer would endanger the local labour market.'[18]

For Ashbee, never a man of half-measures, saw in the move to Campden an opportunity to revive the educational aspects of his work; using a disused malt-house as his school premises he invited the local people, both adult and children, to acquire skills 'such as are not provided in the Campden Elementary Schools, or for which the schools have no conveniences, namely: swimming, gardening, cookery, carpentry, life and duties of the citizen'.[19] He also organized Oxford University extension classes and summer schools, and persuaded his friends to lecture there. In 1905, for example, Walter Crane was talking on *Design in Relation to the Crafts*, and Edward Carpenter on *Small Holdings and Life on the Land*. Ashbee also revived dying crafts such as lead glazing, and photographs in *Craftsmanship in Competitive Industry* show the other activities that the Guild promoted: domestic science classes, drama, physical jerks, the brass band and swimming galas are all recorded. If the physical drill brigade look somewhat incongruous in their flat caps, dark suits, stiff collars, white shirts and ties, this is no doubt due to the newly acquired skills of the ladies, who were taught starching in their laundry classes—Ashbee having discovered that 'when the folk of Campden want their shirts and collars starched they have to send them by carrier to Evesham'.[20]

So for a brief period at least, Ashbee was fulfilling all his aims, and contemporary accounts give a glowing picture of life at Campden. 'When I saw the workshops', wrote Charles Rowley in *A Workshop Paradise*[21] '. . . one could readily imagine that they were native to the place. An old mill with a ground and upper storey lends itself to handicraft workshops of this nature. Every window looks out onto a lovely common garden, every bench has a posy on it. Nothing could be more delightful than to be doing rationally good work in such surroundings.'

The exodus to Chipping Campden, however, marked the beginning of the Guild's decline; in 1907, when the ideals for the *Deutscher Werkbund* were being formulated, Ashbee was faced with financial crises and dwindling markets, and in 1908 'after three years of acute commercial depression and heavy losses'[22] the Guild was dissolved and reconstructed as a trust, many of its members were laid off and it survived precariously until the outbreak of war in 1914.

What had gone wrong? Ashbee himself believed that he could identify several causes for the failure. He realized that the beginning of the decline had coincided with the Guild's move to the country and the economic depression that had accompanied it. When the workshops were in London these 'lean years' were not so crippling, since his craftsmen could, if the worse came to the worst, find alternative employment until better times. In the country, however, there was no such choice; Ashbee had hoped that the cultivation of allotments would enable his workmen to be more or less self-supporting, but not many rejoiced at the idea of living from the land, which, of course, is easier said than done; cottages were hard to come by and in urgent need of repair, and because of the difficulties of transport and the high charges on the railways, links with London, which were vital to the Guild, were difficult to maintain.

These were immediate and practical problems, but Ashbee also had to contend with local indifference to his work which was intensified by the fashion for 'antiques' ('turned out' as he put it 'in hundreds to the hum of the latest American machinery');[23] he found his clients unwilling to pay the rate for the job, especially when 'dear Emily' as Ashbee and his companions called their amateur competitor, was always 'tingling to sell her work before she half knows how to make it', charging 2d an hour for her labour, where the 'skilled workman has to sell his for 1s in order to keep up standard and support his family.'[24]

In 1908, however, Ashbee was still convinced that the ideology that had inspired his enterprise was sound, and that some form of guild or co-operative system could and should be established to meet contemporary industrial needs. It was only within such a system, he believed, that individuality and freedom of expression could be preserved; any compromise with the contemporary industrial set-up would bring about the total extinction of leisure and of culture. He wrote in *Craftsmanship and Competitive Industry*:

'If we have decided no longer to rebel against the Industrial system, which chains us together, but to quietly and firmly set to work and reconstruct it (abandoning the position of Morris and Ruskin for instance—the intellectual Ludditism) . . . we find industrial organisation ever screwing down and screwing down, we find the drive severer, the competition keener, we find industrial democracy ever closing in . . . the levelling and uniformity more necessary, more terrible. What becomes of the individual, of what weight is the little human soul upon this dark archangel's scale?'

Three years later, however, when he published *Should we stop teaching Art?* Ashbee's attitude had changed, and the extent of this change is reflected in the first 'axiom' upon which the book was based. 'Modern civilization', wrote Ashbee, 'rests on machinery, and no system for the endowment, or the encouragement, or the teaching of art can be sound that does not recognize this.'[25]

Although these opinions were not entirely iconoclastic, they obviously represent a radical reappraisal of fundamental assumptions on Ashbee's part. The reasons for so dramatic a conversion could perhaps be attributed to the climate of opinion, or to Ashbee's response to the failure of the Guild. It is very tempting to assume, however, that Ashbee revised his attitudes as a direct result of his various visits to America, the intellectual challenge of his friendship with Frank Lloyd Wright and his knowledge and study of Wright's theory and writing.

Frank Lloyd Wright

Ashbee visited the States several times; his first visit was in 1896, and his experiences at that time only served to reinforce his belief in the craft ideal. In New York, for example, he spent a day 'going over works and workshops' and was 'wearied with many hours of commercialism and shown endless symbols of waste and luxury— nothing that revealed any joy in the producer or character in the product'.[26] He admired Cornel University, but was appalled by the Drexel Institute in Philadelphia, where the curator had shown him a Doulton vase—in Ashbee's opinion an 'abomination'—and had never heard of William De Morgan. He visited a metalwork factory, but the only design he could find to admire was a simply hammered vessel; he told the designers it was the best metalwork he had seen in the States, but they laughed and advised him 'not to tell the boss', since it was expensive and 'quite unsaleable'.

His next visit, in 1900–1, however, was to prove more challenging. This was a fund-raising lecture tour, sponsored by the National Trust, and Ashbee went aiming to 'tilt at the great industrial windmill'. His first impressions were negative; he saw himself 'pleading for a cause not so much lost as forgotten' and declared that the crafts in America 'no longer served any purpose'. 'Furniture,' he wrote, 'metalwork, the things of the house, jewelry, the hand-printed book, modern design . . . such things in the new world were done by the machine,' and badly done, since 'the machine in its relation to life is not so much hostile as unintelligent'.[27] For consolation he visited the graves of Emerson and Thoreau, and he stayed with Dr Emerson, the son of Ralph Waldo, at his house near Concord, admiring an educational system which allowed 'all the Concord children, boys and girls to learn together . . . everyone standing an equal chance'. He saw the Roycrofters at work, and was not impressed; but he also met a 'young press runner, Mr Rogers, head of the Riverside Press, who . . . is fighting the old battle of commercial v. artistic success, and trying to put some spirit of good into the stacks of trade printing he had to do'.[28] His most momentous encounter, however, was with Frank Lloyd Wright.

Ashbee first met Wright, who was just then turned thirty, in Chicago in December 1900; he was therefore one of the first Europeans to see and comment on his work, and to single him out from the groups working in Chicago at this time. Ashbee was staying at Hull House, a far more invigorating proposition, he found, than Toynbee Hall; it had, he felt, an eager corporate spirit, 'a capacity for enjoyment' and a far more realistic awareness of the problems of city life than its British counterpart. Chicago itself he found at once dynamic and horrifying.

'Smoke, darkness, noise: the clashing of car bells, engine bells, steamer bells; the grating of endless trolleys as they dash along the street, the shriek of the AMERICAN VOICE trying to make itself heard above the uproar. The rattle and thunder of the elevated railway, the unearthly buzzing of electric cabs, and the thudding of the power houses that shake a whole street.'[29]

Ashbee obviously found Wright and his colleagues as bewildering and as stimulating as the city itself, but he was shrewd enough to recognize the force and potential of Wright's personality. 'Wright', he wrote from Chicago, 'is far and away the ablest man in our line of work that I have come across in Chicago, perhaps in America. He not only has ideas, but the power of expressing them, and his Husser House, over which he took me, showing me every detail with the keenest delight, is one of the most beautiful and individual creations I have seen in America.'[30] The Husser House, which was designed in 1899, was typical of Wright's Chicago houses of the 1890s; it was a long, horizontal structure, built in brick, with the characteristic Sullivan-inspired terracotta decoration beneath the eaves. Its living areas, dining-room and living-room, each with their own fireplace, were interconnecting and were all on the first storey, to give the occupants a view of Lake Michigan. An architectural solution of this kind, individual, traditional, yet with radical elements, sympathetic both to the site and the materials used, with its hints both of Voysey and the Japanese, could not have failed to impress Ashbee, who would be aware both of the inspiration and the intellect that formed it.

For Wright, who was of course familiar with the work of Ruskin and Morris,* shared his radicalism, his mistrust of '*Beaux-Arts* intellectualism' and certain convictions concerning the nature of architecture with the British Arts and Crafts Movement. When he wrote (in *A Testament*) that 'The artist-architect will be a man inspired by love of the nature of nature, knowing that man is not made for architecture; architecture is made for man'[31] he was speaking the language of Morris, Ashbee, Webb and Lethaby. A common ground had been prepared by the general interchange of ideas throughout the century, and the links between the British and the American Arts and Crafts movement were reinforced by publications such as *The*

* Writing, for example, in *A Testament* about his early years in Chicago he said 'Good William Morris and John Ruskin were much in evidence in Chicago intellectual circles at the time'.

*Craftsman.** As far as Wright was concerned, however, the resemblances between the two ideologies were only superficial, and Ashbee was to find that Wright, in this instance, regarded him more as a challenge than as an ally in the same cause.

'He threw down the glove to me in characteristic Chicagoan manner', writes Ashbee, 'when we discussed the Arts and Crafts. "My God", he said, "is machinery, and the art of the future will be the expression of the individual artist through the thousand powers of the machine—the machine doing all those things that the individual workman cannot do. The creative artist is the man who controls all this and understands it." '[32]

Wright was obviously using Ashbee as a sounding board for his lecture *The Art and Craft of the Machine* which he delivered in Hull House in 1901. In pronouncing the machine 'the normal tool of our civilization' Wright was, in effect, bridging the gulf between the nineteenth and the twentieth century, and in insisting that 'genius must dominate the work of the contrivance it has created' he was paving the way for the doctrinal dilemmas of the Modern Movement. It was to be several years, however, before this text reached Europe, and at this stage, as far as Ashbee was concerned, the challenge, though remarkable enough to write about in his journal, went no further than a conversational sparring match between two architects. Wright, Ashbee noted 'was surprised to find how much I concurred with him, but I added the rider that the individuality of the average had to be considered, in addition to that of the artistic creator himself'.[33] This concern for the welfare of the workman, especially when the 'artistic creator' proclaimed his God to be machinery, was of course to be expected from a champion of the English Arts and Crafts ideals. Nevertheless Ashbee realized that the American city created new problems, which would need new men and new solutions:

'Yes, it was the great drive, the strain and stress of this terrible and wonderful city that set him moving with the rest, and I am not sure that strong as he is, he will ultimately be able to give that expression to his ideas of which he is capable and worthy. He introduced me to his master, Sullivan, in whom the Chicago spirit finds such anxious and restless expression. Wright is greater than his master, and will become the leader, if he is not that already, of the little group of artists, architects for the most part, whom he has around him . . . Chicago's burning activity kindles such brotherhood with a flame peculiarly its own.'[34]

Ashbee himself returned to England, and to Chipping Campden, greeting the green fields and farmsteads with relief. In 1908, however, after the reconstruction of the original Guild, he returned to the States again, lecturing on such subjects as the *Arts and Crafts and Education* and the *Arts and Crafts and the Spirit of Socialism* to 'enthusiastic audiences' in Montana and Stanford. He also renewed his friendship

* Edited by Gustave Stickley and published in Syracuse, New York from 1902 to 1932, this magazine, as well as promoting Stickley's interpretation of the English ideals, became to a certain extent the mouthpiece of the Chicago school; Louis Sullivan, for example, published his article *What is Architecture?, A Study of the American people today* in the magazine in 1906.

with Frank Lloyd Wright, and in spite of differences of temperament and ideals, the two men were obviously mutually sympathetic, since their correspondence continued in a sporadic fashion until 1938.[35] Wright in fact stayed with the Ashbees in Chipping Campden in September 1910, and it was probably during this visit that he asked Ashbee to write the introduction to the second Wasmuth edition of his work, which was published in Berlin in 1911. (This publication virtually introduced Wright to Europe since the first Wasmuth folio was produced in an expensive and limited edition.) Ashbee, therefore, must have been working on the introduction while he was preparing *Should We Stop Teaching Art?*, and the need to define his attitudes to Wright, together with his knowledge of Wright's *In the Cause of Architecture*, which was published in 1908, and from which he quotes in his Wasmuth introduction, no doubt contributed to certain fundamental changes of attitude expressed in Ashbee's own book.

Not that Ashbee adopts a sycophantic attitude to Wright; in fact the two seemed to have been on the verge of a quarrel during Wright's visit, one main bone of contention apparently being Ashbee's attitude to the Japanese influence on Wright's work.[36] Nor was Ashbee wholeheartedly in favour of Wright's approach. 'I have seen buildings of Frank Lloyd Wright's', he wrote in the introduction, 'that I would like to touch with the enchanted wand; not to alter their structure in plan or form, or carcass, but to clothe them with a more living and tender detail.'[37] He insisted, however, that the importance of Wright lay in his 'determination, amounting sometimes to heroism, to master the machine and use it at all costs to find the forms and treatment it might render without the abuse of tradition' and that 'one recognises in his architecture the struggle for mastery of the machine, and that is the true province of his powers'.[38]

Ashbee praised American architects' willingness to experiment with new materials and their intelligent use of machine techniques; he also admired the 'democracy' of the American architectural spirit, which, he said, found expression in office buildings, libraries, clubs, schools and universities—a theme he also stresses in *Should We Stop Teaching Art?*, when he contrasts the American and British approach to architectural problems. 'With us', he wrote, 'Architecture is, so to speak, a traditional luxury, in which a wealthy university or wealthy individual may indulge, but in which the people share less and less; in America, it is more of a democratic need for which provision has to be made.' 'In America', he continued, 'there is a greater sweep, a more logical planning, a wider outlook, a more conscious grasp of the coming needs of the community, and more specific handling of industrial methods. There may not be the tender solicitude as with us for aesthetic traditions, nor the same taste or feeling or refinement, but the loss of these is atoned for in the fulfilment of other, and for the moment, greater needs.'[39] He quotes the Larkin Building as an example of how architecture can meet the needs of contemporary society, describes how the Chicago architects 'largely inspired by Frank Lloyd Wright' are solving the problem of art and machinery, and in a chapter headed 'How we should set about to eliminate ugliness' states that we 'should study the conditions in Germany and America, where they are in many ways more advanced than we are in treating the problem of the Arts as a social matter—a part of life'.

Should We Stop Teaching Art?, as Ashbee explains in his introduction, was intended to be part of a larger work called *The Man and the Machine*, which would discuss the general problem of the 'Arts under Mechanical Conditions'. He wrote it at a time when there was yet another crisis in the art schools, so that the book was, to a certain extent, a personal analysis of the nature and purpose of art education. Characteristically, he insists that art education has failed because its organizers have ignored one of the fundamentals of Ruskin's teaching, namely that 'we cannot teach Art as an abstract skill or power. It is a result of a certain ethical state of the nation'. And he linked the failure of the art schools with that of the Arts and Crafts movement, whose principles, he maintained, were 'more consistently and logically studied in Germany and America'. His ideal would have been to see the preservation and extension of guild and workshop techniques in the craft-based industries, while in the heavier industries 'the more the machine is used the better'. He believed that the art schools would serve a more realistic purpose if they were reorganized as guild-type workshops, the students serving an apprenticeship before being accepted for a 'trade', but at the same time he urged that the schools should establish more valid links with industry, their rôle being to establish standards and advise on models for standardization.

There are obvious links here with Gropius's ideals for the Bauhaus when he first established the school in Weimar, and although Ashbee does not mention the *Deutscher Werkbund* which had been established four years earlier, his recommendations bear a close relationship to *Werkbund* thinking. For by 1911 Ashbee can no longer deny the machine-made object an aesthetic value, nor does he believe that the 'beauty' of the machine product should relate to that of its craft equivalent:

'It is often supposed that there cannot be beautiful machine products, or that the beauty of a mechanical object lies in its conformity to the standard of a hand-made piece. But experience does not bear out this supposition. In modern mechanical industry "standard" is necessary, and "standardisation" is necessary. The principle in each is sound and the community needs both.'

Ashbee's reference to standards and standardization and their relationship to the crafts and industry is very Muthesian, as is his new found conviction that the survival of arts can only be achieved through an understanding and acceptance of economic and technical change. 'If we want the Arts', he maintained, 'we must enable them to meet the new industrial and economic conditions of our time.' He insisted that the whole problem of architectural as well as design training should be re-examined; architecture, he said 'should be studied both as an Art and a Science', and should concentrate on 'modern mechanical industry' rather than being confused 'as it is at present with painting or with Arts and Crafts'. Craftsmanship, however, would still play a key role in both design and architectural training, since it would provide 'the grammar of the Industrial Arts, Architecture and Industry'.

There are, of course, inconsistencies and elements of the quixotic here, but Ashbee tempered these with much sound sense, especially when he called for a more realistic and systematic form of architectural training; he also anticipated the contemporary preoccupation with cataloguing systems when he pointed to the need for a rationalization of material relating to the building trade: 'If I were to let the catalogues, calendars, circulars, advertisements and letters of enquiry accumulate as they litter into my office from week to week, I should, after a few months, not be able to enter it at all . . . There should be a proper sorting, grading and testing of all this building trade matter.' He was also moving towards the conception of the designer as a problem solver rather than as a creator of beautiful objects—a conception that was latent at the Bauhaus and fundamental to the teaching at Ulm, and one that contemporary art education has only just begun to grasp. 'What the manufacturers themselves often fail to see,' he pointed out, 'for their point of view is much limited to the study of their own processes, is that the mechanical system in many directions has come to an end, that here and there it has reached a point where it can go no further, and that progress and profit can now often be made only by organisation, concentration, combined finance and the cutting of certain mechanical processes altogether.' He quotes Veblen's *Theory of Business Enterprise*, published in 1904, to support him, and suggests that industry needs the services of men who will act both as watch-dogs and advisers—anticipating in some measure the post-war consumer movements and the work of organizations such as the Svenska Slöjdförenigen and the British Council of Industrial Design.

In 1911 Ashbee was confident that Britain had the potential to face the problems of mass production; the men were there, he said, and so were the machines, 'but we have not yet found the right way of using either'. 'The right way' had, by this time, been diligently sought after for nearly a century, but before the outbreak of war it was generally assumed by British theorists that in spite of all their endeavours, the Germans and the Americans were nearer to finding a solution than they were. For as Morris had once pointed out 'a reform in art which is founded on individualism must perish with the individuals who have set it going'; and this, it seemed, was to be the fate of the British movement which in spite, or perhaps because of its social preoccupations, relied on individual rather than collective solutions. The most urgent task for the twentieth century, therefore, was to reconcile the claims of the individual with the requirements of the mass market, to equate subjectivity with standardization, and, in effect, to apply the Arts and Crafts ideals of fitness and truth to material to the machine-made product. The British acknowledged their dilemma; they could diagnose their sickness, but they could not cure it, and to them it seemed that the Germans had become their torch-bearers. For the Germans were formulating ideals both for architecture and design that made sense on every level—social, economic and aesthetic.

7 Towards an efficiency style

In their efforts to effect a union between art and industry, British design reformers had several times throughout the nineteenth century turned to Germany for both precept and example. The Arts and Crafts generation, however, tended by its very nature to insularity, and its members rarely looked to contemporary achievements abroad for instruction or inspiration. When, like Ashbee, they began to do so, it was because they saw in American and Continental developments a valid extension of the craft ideal, rather than a complete break with the values that they had established. The humanizing of technology, therefore, and the harnessing of its achievements to social ends became the primary concern of the twentieth-century inheritors of Morris's ideals, and on this basic level there are obvious similarities between British theory, and that, for example, of Le Corbusier and Gropius. The first two decades of the twentieth century, however, were to culminate in a sense of frustration and lack of achievement on the part of British designers and design theorists. They were, after all, unlike their Continental counterparts, inheritors of values that had been established by an earlier generation, rather than pioneers of new ideas, and when they attempted to translate these values into corporate, rather than individual endeavour they met with little response. The garden city movement, for example, now considered as valid a solution to the problem of suburban living as say, Weissenhof, had a tepid reception, and, to some critics at least, the idea of the 'New Town' seemed at best a ludicrously Utopian concept. ('We have got to make the best of our existing cities,' said the *Fabian News* reviewer of Howard's *Tomorrow: a Peaceful Path to Real Reform*, 'and proposals for building new ones are about as useful as would be arrangements for protection against visits from Mr Wells's Martians.'[1]) Again, the most significant architectural contribution at the turn of the century came from Mackintosh, whose genius the majority of his contemporaries failed to acknowledge. And if Continental designers enthused about British applied design they were not, paradoxically, so much concerned with those areas (other than printing and typography) that had preoccupied the Arts and Crafts movement, but with British boots and shoes, leather work, sports equipment and plumbing—areas, in fact, in which a tradition of British quality and practicality had been established.[2] For, as Lethaby was to point out: 'We do not allow shoddy in cricket or football, but reserve it for serious things like houses and books, furniture and funerals.'[3] And in this context, it is perhaps significant that Lethaby, who made the most important contribution to British design and architectural theory during this period, failed, unlike Gropius and Le Corbusier, to produce a radical architecture to match it, and the Bauhaus succeeded, where the British Arts and Crafts schools failed, in establishing valid links with industry.

Lethaby and the Central School

Lethaby, nevertheless, is a far from negligible figure, and until the Bauhaus was established, his Central School was considered the most progressive art school in Europe. (Muthesius, for example, cited it as the 'best organised contemporary art school'.[4])

It was founded in 1896 when Lethaby, then aged thirty-nine, had been working as Norman Shaw's right-hand man for almost seventeen years; he was one of the initiators of the Art-Workers' Guild, whose ideals the school attempted to realize, and from whose membership most of the staff was drawn, and for two years before the school was founded he and George Frampton,[5] his co-principal in the early years, had been acting as art advisers to the Technical Education Board of the then London County Council, the sponsors of the school. According to the Board's Report for 1895–6, the aim of its new school was to encourage the 'industrial application of decorative design'; first and foremost, however, it was a school of craftsmanship— its pupils went there to make, not draw, and it was for this reason, the Board insisted, that 'admission to the school is only extended to those actually engaged in one or other of the crafts, and the school makes no provision for the amateur student of drawing or painting'.[6]

In Lethaby's new school, therefore, drawing and painting were taught, not as ends in themselves, but as part of a training in craftsmanship; again Lethaby insisted that all his staff were practising designers, and he campaigned for the right to employ part-time teachers, so that designers could, without abandoning their profession, convey something of its practical realities to their students. During its first twelve years the school was housed in makeshift premises in Upper Regent Street. Here 'listeners to Halsey Ricardo's lectures would perforce sit there with their umbrellas up',[7] but physical discomforts did not detract from the sense of achievement, for staff and students alike experienced the reality of Lethaby's vision of a new unity between hand and brain. Priscilla Johnston's biography of her father conveys something of the atmosphere of Central life at this time:

'This building was a kind of improvisation consisting of two houses joined together by a dilapidated conservatory, full of odd corners, creaking wooden staircases and small rooms packed as full as they could hold with eager students. Over it presided Lethaby who had brought it into being and who must have filled it with an extraordinary sense of unity, for all, staff and students alike, were united in their love for him. His staff, it was said, never felt that they were working *under* him, but *with* him: even the students felt themselves to be pioneers taking part in an exciting experiment.'[8]

Because it was an experimental school working towards the realization of Arts and

Crafts ideals, Lethaby was able to gather together a distinguished staff. In the early years, as well as Halsey Ricardo, who lectured on architecture, there was R. Catterson-Smith who taught wallpaper and textile design (he was to become director of the Birmingham School of Art); Frank Morley Fletcher, later director of the Edinburgh College of Art, specialized in the wood-cut; Douglas Cockerell, who joined the staff in 1897, taught book-binding (he had learned the craft from Cobden-Sanderson and was to become adviser to W. H. Smith & Son, whose partner, St. John Hornby, was one of the first patrons of Eric Gill). In 1899 Edward Johnston began to teach himself and his students 'illuminating and lettering as an art'. ('Johnston's students', wrote his daughter, 'had every reason to regard themselves as pioneers. There was no question of his playing the expert; he told them how little he knew and how much there was to discover and enlisted their help.') In addition F. W. Troup, an architect who taught lead-casting was assisted by W. Dodds—plumber: 'the latter a description of an instructor's qualification unlike at that time to be found in the prospectus of any other art school'.[9]

After its move to new and purpose-built premises in Southampton Row in 1908, the school was able to establish five major departments, each devoted to the traditional Arts and Crafts specializations. By 1914, for example, when Fred Burridge was Principal, the first floor was 'practically a self-contained school devoted to the work of the silversmith and the allied crafts of the goldsmith and jeweller, including diamond mounting, gem-setting, chasing, engraving, die-sinking, repoussé work, metal casting and enamelling';[10] the furniture department was on the third floor, and one of the instructors here was George Jack, of the Morris Firm; there was a section devoted to dress design, embroidery and needlework, while the stained-glass students working 'in beautifully lighted classrooms on the top floor' were 'carefully instructed in the technicalities peculiar to their branch of the arts'.[11]

The department whose work was to have the most influence, however, throughout Europe as well as in England, was that of book design and printing, which had grown from Johnston's preoccupation with lettering. This was set up in 1905 at the request of Emery Walker and T. J. Cobden-Sanderson; J. H. Mason, chief compositor at the Doves Press, was appointed first instructor in printing, and by 1914 a book could be 'produced in its studios complete in every respect—printing, illustrations and binding'.[12] As well as the staff—Johnston himself, Mason and Douglas Cockerell—their students, including Eric Gill, Noel Rooke, Graily Hewitt, Anna Simons (and Cobden-Sanderson who joined Johnston's class at the age of sixty) were all exploring and extending the pioneer work of Emery Walker and the Kelmscott Press, and thus consolidating Britain's reputation as pioneers in the twentieth-century revival in book production. Johnston, however, was at first reluctant to extend his interest beyond lettering to typography; his objections to designing type, according to his daughter, arose from his conviction that 'an object could only properly be designed by the craftsman who made it because the design should be the outcome of the craft itself and not arbitrarily determined on a drawing board. Thus he considered that the proper person to design type was the punch-cutter.' His resolution was cracked, however, by the enthusiasm of Count Kessler, who as early as 1910 was planning the *Hamlet* that was to be printed by his Cranach Press in Weimar eighteen years later. Johnston, working in collaboration with Edward Prince, who had cut Morris's *Golden* type, designed types for Kessler, and the fact that the latter came to England for his craftsmen (Edward Gordon Craig produced the wood-cut illustrations, G. T. Friend completed the cutting after Prince's death, while J. H. Mason supervised the type-setting and printing) is a tribute to Britain's reputation in this field. In fact, when Bernard Newdigate visited the exhibition of Graphic Arts in Leipzig just before the outbreak of the war he reported seeing 'the hand of Johnston on every stall and on every wall'.[13]

In England, however, not all Johnston's enterprises were meeting with immediate acclaim, and the magazine *Imprint*, which had been founded by Gerard Meynell in 1912, and which he edited together with Ernest Jackson and J. H. Mason, survived for less than a year. Collaboration with Meynell, however, led to Johnston's meeting Frank Pick, and the commission to design the type-face for London's Underground. Johnston, therefore, the total purist who had dedicated his career to *Writing, Illuminating and Lettering*[14] became one of the founders of modern typography. 'He approached the problem', wrote his daughter, 'with the austerity of an engineer'; his primary concern was with legibility, and because he believed that legibility was linked with familiarity, he based the new face on what he defined as 'classical Roman capital proportions'; starting from this premise, he insisted, 'the alphabet designed itself'. Eric Gill, whose *Gill Sans* was designed for the Monotype Corporation in 1928, frankly acknowledged his debt to Johnston's London Underground type, and so it can be claimed that Johnston, the calligrapher, changed the face of modern commercial printing.

This, according to Lethaby, was the way matters should be organized, the craft (representing the union between hand and brain) inspiring the machine, and it is significant that it was for *Imprint* that he wrote *Art and Workmanship*, the essay most frequently quoted in connection with his work and his ideals. 'A work of art', he wrote in this essay, 'is first of all a well-made thing. It may be a well-made statue or a well-made chair, or a well-made book . . . Most simply and generally art may be thought of as *the well doing of what needs doing*.' And again 'The master-workman, further, must have control from first to last to shape and finish as he will. If I were asked for some simple test by which we might hope to know a work of art when we saw one, I should suggest something like this: *Every work of art shows that it was made by a human being for a human being*.'[15] This basic and deceptively simple humanism, therefore, was the cornerstone upon which Lethaby based his design philosophy; design, for him, was concerned with people, and no one, theorist or practitioner, would get very far if he ignored this basic fact. 'I don't believe in genius one bit,' he wrote, 'nor anything else abnormal. I want the common-place.'[16] Lethaby's commonplace, however, like Webb's, reflected the highest rather than the lowest common denominator. It represented common sense and practicality and assumed the existence of a kind of folk-knowledge or instinct concerning the way things should be built and made. Such knowledge, however, was in danger of extinction, and it was threatened, not primarily by industrialization but by the pursuit of the phoney and pretentious, by what Lethaby called 'sham artistic twaddle'.[17] 'Don't think of nice drawings or style-names and art talk,' he told the RIBA in 1917, 'but in facts of life and building.'[18] Art, he insisted, was 'a natural human aptitude which has been explained almost out of existence'[19] and 'the long word Architecture has destroyed the art of building'.[20] For although Lethaby spent his formative years working for Norman Shaw, it was Ruskin, Morris and above all Philip Webb whom he acknowledged as his 'workmasters'.[21] He paid his tribute to Webb in the biography that was first published in serial form in *The Builder* in 1925,[22] and the virtues he ascribed to Webb reflect Lethaby's own ideals, for it was Webb, he said, who taught him that 'architecture was not designs, forms and grandeur, but buildings, honest and human, with hearts in them'.

To Lethaby, therefore, the past was a living book from which architects could learn the facts both of life and design; unlike many of his contemporaries on the Continent he did not believe that the new century had created new men, and if it had introduced new materials these must be used in the service of humanity rather than as a demonstration of the alien concept of 'modernity'. His teaching at the Central School, therefore, was based on the axiom 'Would you know the new, you must search the old',[23] and like Morris, he acclaimed the work of the Society for the Protection of Ancient Buildings, not because it was 'engaged in an intense study of antiquity' but because it 'became a school of rational builders and modern building'.[24] And so it was totally in character that, having spent some twenty years teaching design at the Central School and the Royal College of Art, he also spent twenty years as surveyor of the fabric of Westminster Abbey, and that his numerous publications should include titles such as *Lead Work Old and Ornamental and for the most part English* (1893), *Westminster Abbey and the King's Craftsmen* (1906), *Greek Buildings represented by Fragments in the British Museum* (1923), as well as his better-known collected essays *Form in Civilisation* (1922), his *Architecture, Mysticism and Myth* (1892) and the Home University Library *Architecture* (1911). For Lethaby was a scholar as well as a champion of the past (like Morris he apparently astounded the experts by his ability to date and identify their fragments and specimens).[25] Again, like Morris, his scholarship did not lead him to promote book-learning as an end in itself: he condemned any form of education, from the infant school up, that put 'subjects in place of substances',[26] and he attempted, with little success, to abolish the examination system at the Central School. ('In a practical matter like art', he wrote, 'we might even hope to break through the mystery mongering of educationists and their pathetic belief in written papers.')[27] His concern was with a living tradition in the practise of design and architecture, not with the academic 'disease of unreality' that had destroyed the art schools, and his absorption with 'architecture as a direct and developing art'[28] was to lead him to a functionalist conception of design that had similarities with that of the *Werkbund*, Le Corbusier and Gropius. For since art and architecture were 'practical matters' it followed that science had as vital a rôle to play in their development as tradition: thus Lethaby came to insist that 'architects must be trained as engineers are trained'[29] and to regret that his knowledge of 'steel and concrete construction' was so much more scanty than his knowledge of Cathedral building.[30]

Lethaby's insistence that 'the living stem of building design can only be found by following the scientific method'[31] became more emphatic in the years leading up to World War I, and by 1920, three years before the publication of Le Corbusier's *Vers une Architecture* he is declaring that ' "House like" should express as much as "ship-shape". Our airplanes and motors and even bicycles are in their way perfect. We need to bring this ambition for perfect solutions into housing of all sorts and scales.'[32] 'The house of the future', he wrote in another essay in that same year, 'will be designed as a ship is designed, as an organism which has to function properly in all its parts.'[33]

The task facing the new generation, therefore, was to bridge the gulf between art and science, to equate art with practicality and to create 'an efficiency style'.[34]

The possibility of Britain ever being able to achieve this, however, seemed remote. Even before World War I created its own crises the British economy had begun to decline: British industrialists were no longer self-confident pioneers, and Germany and America were well ahead in the race for 'modernization' and technical progress. While the Edwardian age produced its architecture of conspicuous consumption—banks, luxury hotels, prestige office blocks, country houses and public schools—Edwardian industry was realizing too late the cost of resting on its laurels. The staple industries of Britain—coal, cotton and shipbuilding—were entering their steady decline; the metal industries of the West Midlands could no longer rely on a stable home market to keep their enterprise afloat, and the depression which had destroyed Ashbee's Guild of Handicraft brought with it grinding poverty for both country and town. Faced with these crises, the flirtations between 'art' and industry ceased. The consumer goods industries, no longer able to compete with Germany and America, concentrated their attention on the less sophisticated and demanding markets of Asia and Africa. Neither the South Kensington nor the Morris inspired campaigns for design reform had succeeded in influencing the 'taste' of the masses; the museums and art galleries, conceived as places where the workman and his employer might spend happy hours in self-improvement, became shrines for the connoisseur and the scholar; in school 'art' was (and too often still is) a subject for the intellectual lightweight, the lesser being who could not cope with an academic or athletic course; the art school, in spite of the revitalizing efforts of Lethaby and his followers, still ranked as a poor second best to the university, or as a useful finishing school for one's girls. The situation seemed even more desperate than in 1835, and the suggested remedies had, in fact, analogies with the earlier experience, for it was generally assumed among the new generation concerned with design reform that the key to future progress lay within industry, rather than with the craftsman. The catalysts on this occasion were the financial failure, in 1912, of an Arts and Crafts Exhibition Society display, and the resounding success of the *Werkbund*'s exhibition in Cologne in 1914. Some of the members of the Arts and Crafts Society had been to Cologne, and it was largely as a result of their reactions to this experience that the Design and Industries Association was formed in 1915 to promote 'a more intelligent demand amongst the public for what is best and soundest in design' as well as the idea that 'many machine processes tend to certain qualities of their own'.[35] The founder members of the DIA included Ambrose Heal and Harry Peach, both designers and retailers, J. H. Mason from the London Central School, and Harold Stabler, the silversmith who at that time was teaching at the Royal College of Art; Lethaby and Benson gave them their full support, and the association began, even during the war years, to attempt 'to come to terms with design in all our industries'.[36]

It was, however, with some irony that these early DIA members acknowledged, as Ashbee had done some three years earlier, that British precept had inspired German practice, and that ideals formulated over two generations in England were evidently to be realized, with a seemingly remarkable rapidity and efficiency, by the Germans.

European interpretations

The history of Hermann Muthesius' mission to England is now a familiar one; he was attached to the German embassy in London with a brief to report on the progress of British architecture, and his stay lasted seven years. When he returned in 1903, he began to write extensively about British architecture and design (the three-volume *Das Englische Haus* was published in 1905). His stay in London, however, had coincided with the launching of both the Austrian and the German Secession movements; in 1895 Otto Wagner, newly appointed as professor of architecture at the Academy in Vienna had declared in his inaugural lecture that 'all modern forms must correspond to new materials and the new requirements of our time, if they are to fit modern mankind'.[37] The Wiener Secession was officially launched in 1897; Olbrich designed its exhibition building in 1898, and subsequent Secession exhibitions gave pride of place to British work, notably that of Mackintosh. In 1903, for example, when Josef Hoffmann launched the *Wiener Werkstätten*, he modelled them on Ashbee's Guild of Handicraft. By this time, however, similar organizations were already flourishing in Germany. The *Deutsche Werkstätten für Kunst und Handwerk* were founded in Munich in 1897; Dresden established *Werkstätten* the following year and by 1914 there were *Werkstätten* in Hellerau, Berlin and Hanover. In the early years the founder members of these groups, who included Richard Riemerschmid, August Endell and Peter Behrens, were working in the *Secession* or *Jugendstil*, and the British arts and crafts designers, epitomizing the fruitful union of *Kunst* and *Handwerk*, were encouraged to contribute to *Werkstätte* displays. As early as 1904, however, Riemerschmid, with his brother-in-law Karl Schmidt, was exhibiting machine-made furniture, and by 1914 German *Typenmöbel*—made up from mass-produced standardized components—was familiar enough to merit a mention in the *Studio Year-Book*. In the same issue in which the editorial on British developments had deplored 'the lack of originality' in that country's design achievements and had declared that the 'application of art to industry' was a 'matter of vital importance', L. Deubner was writing about the success of the German *Werkbund*, which had been founded seven years earlier, and pre-viewing its forthcoming exhibition in Cologne. He described German progress in the wise use of the machine, demonstrating his point by citing the example of their 'type' furniture, which was being designed, he said, by some twenty architects, including Riemerschmid, Behrens and Adelbert Niemeyer. 'The great economic mode of this type of production', he reported, 'arises from the fact that all these single parts, of which there are something like 800 different kinds, can be made in large quantities and with the most advantageous employment of machine labour, while the extensive range of combinations ensures to the complete article an individuality and character of its own, without betraying the use of machinery in its production.'[38]

The idea that the use of the machine was in some way a betrayal died hard, even in Germany, where a powerful lobby of industrialists were as anxious as the designers and theorists of the *Werkstätten* to establish both practical standards for their activities and a philosophy that would define and justify them. The formation of the *Werkbund* and the subsequent attempts to clarify its goals aimed to provide both standards and a philosophy, but in its early years the *Werkbund* became the focus of a battle of design ideologies which centred round the conflicting claims of the individual versus the mass product, the need to establish a *Zeit* (contemporary) as opposed to a *Jugendstil*, and the need to define this *Zeitstil*. Muthesius, its founder, was, in this first decade, at the storm centre. As a civil servant and a representative of the Prussian Board of Trade he appears to have been realistic, unpretentious and essentially practical, and it was these qualities that he admired in the English. On his return to Germany he condemned his compatriots' efforts to inspire an art-industry, mainly on the grounds that they looked to the past, rather than to the present or to the future for their inspiration, and were thus failing to produce designs that would meet contemporary needs and, equally important, designs that would be exportable. For Muthesius was a businessman as well as a theorist; he was as anxious as any German to establish a sound philosophic context for his countryman's activities, but at the same time he would always insist that the problem must be considered from an economic point of view, and that standards, control and discipline belonged equally to the philosophic and economic realms.

The first confrontation came in 1907 when Muthesius gave a speech to the newly founded Trade School in Berlin in which he condemned contemporary practice for perpetuating outmoded design clichés, rather than demanding products that were appropriate to the time, and in which he called for the spiritualization (*Durchgeistigung*) of form.[39] His criticisms were deeply resented, especially by the Berlin *Kunstgewerbe*, who described him as a pernicious influence, an 'enemy of art' and called for his resignation. A meeting was called to discuss the Muthesius case, and Peter Bruckmann, a cutlery manufacturer, has described the proceedings.[40] Bruckmann explained that he did not know Muthesius at the time, but as a manufacturer (he employed designers such as Riemerschmid (pl 86)) he was impressed by Muthesius' opinions. He went along as a supporter of Muthesius' cause and found two other allies there—Dr Wolf Dohrn of the Dresden *Werkstätten*, and Joseph August Lux, a critic. 'Dohrn, Lux and I', he wrote, 'took on . . . the whole assembly. We were given ten minutes in which to put our case.' He then goes on to summarize his own speech in which he called for a *rapprochement* of artistic and business interests, explaining that his aims were the same as those of Muthesius. 'Our concern today', he said, 'is with new ideas, ideas that have already spread throughout Germany . . . Even if you attempt to drive Herr Muthesius from his post, these ideas will still remain. You are shooting arrows at the sun (cheers). I do not say that Herr Muthesius is the sun (more cheers). No, the sun is the new modern design which will not only liberate fashion, but will become essential to our work and our culture.' Dohrn and Lux supported him with equal fervour, and all three left the meeting in total uproar.

All this took place in June 1907, and the *Werkbund* was formed four months later. Its title, with its stress on 'work' rather than 'art' or 'craft' was intended to convey a spiritual as well as a practical union, and its founder members were equally divided among designer/architects and those representing manufacturing interests. The architects included Peter Behrens who had just been appointed consultant to AEG; Bruno Paul, who had designed *Typenmöbel*, and who, also in 1907, was made head of the Berlin *Gewerbeschule*, Richard Riemerschmid, Theodor Fischer and Adalbert Niemeyer, as well as Josef Hoffmann and Josef Olbrich from the *Wiener Werkstätte*. Bruckmann, the Gebrüder Klingspor, Poeschel und Trepte, the Kunstdruckerei Künstlerbund Karlsruhe, as well as the Munich, Dresden and Vienna *Werkstätten* were among the manufacturers. From its outset, therefore, the *Werkbund* included printers, industrialists, members of the progressive craft organizations and influential young architects, and as such it proved a more vigorous body than the DIA. Proof of this lay in its rising membership figures * (all members were elected, and could in fact be debarred if they failed to maintain the required standards), and in the fact that by 1914 it was able to sponsor an exhibition of the scope and influence of that of Cologne.

It was some time, however, before the polemics of the organization were defined, and even within the *Werkbund*, which was united in its campaign against historicism, there were conflicts concerning its first clearly expressed aim—that of ensuring 'quality' in design and workmanship. The word *Qualität* recurs like a talisman throughout early *Werkbund* writing. The purpose of the organization, according to a programme drawn up in 1910, was to 'select the best in art, industry, craftsmanship and trade. It will co-ordinate all those efforts to achieve quality that are evident in industrial endeavours. It will provide a rallying point for all those who are able and willing to achieve such quality, and for those who recognize design (*gewerbliche Arbeit*) as a part, and no small part of our culture.' [41]

Such a programme, however, had its ambiguities, and these centred round the

---

* In 1908 it had 492 members; in 1912 there were 971; in 1914, 1870 and by 1930 there were 3000. (Figures from *Fünfzig Jahre Deutscher Werkbund*.)

definition of quality, the definition of the artist's rôle in this search for quality, and the exact nature of the artist's contribution to industry. As Secessionists all *Werkbund* theorists took for granted one basic tenet of Arts and Crafts thinking, namely that artists were more than easel painters, and that art should express and embrace the whole of life. Contemporary life, however, was being shaped by revolutions in science and technology; it expressed itself in mass-production, mass communication, new means of transport and expanding cities. And if the artist's function in this changing world was difficult to define, it was even more difficult to establish those qualities that would ensure 'good' design. Various points of view were expressed: Friedrich Naumann, for example, in the *Werkbund Yearbook* for 1913 declared that 'taste' was a personal matter, so subjective that no one could presume to state categorically what was good and what was bad. The *Werkbund*, he declared, condemned that which was obviously bad, but would never set out to sponsor one specific style; it was against a 'thoughtless conglomeration of alien components in design', and was striving for unity in domestic design, architecture and fashion.[42] This, of course, was close to British arts and crafts thinking, which did not seek to impose a 'style' but assumed that appropriate forms would emerge if the artist had proper regard for materials and function. (Assumptions that were shared by Gropius when he founded the *Bauhaus*.)

Riemerschmid, who also made an important contribution to *Werkbund* theory, accepted this basic premise. 'Life, not art, creates style,' he wrote.[43] 'It is not made, it grows.' His conviction that 'every epoch creates its own style' led him, like Ruskin and Morris before him, to condemn contemporary society; our cities, our streets, our household equipment, our luxuries and those things we call 'art', he wrote, all these betray our meanness and vulgarity. You will never find 'art', he insisted, where artists have been at work. This statement, however, marks his transition from nineteenth- to twentieth-century attitudes, for Riemerschmid looked to the dockyards and the factories, rather than to the past, for his sources of modern design: liners, aircraft, machinery, technical structures, he declared, revealed forms that were 'taut, austere, confident and unpretentious', forms, in fact, that were truly expressive of the epoch that had created them.

There are obvious analogies here with Loos, with the Futurists, and above all with Le Corbusier's *Vers une Architecture*.[44] Corbusier, of course, was familiar with *Werkbund* thinking, for when the Art School in his native Chaux-de-Fonds had sent him to Germany in 1910 to study German architecture and design, he had worked for a few months with Gropius and Mies van der Rohe in Behrens' office, and he had also spent some time with the *Werkstätte* at Hellerau, where Karl Schmidt and Heinrich Tessenow, both *Werkbund* members, were planning their garden city. *Vers une Architecture*, could, in fact, be described as a *Werkbund* document, for although few of its members would have gone so far as to declare that engineers are 'healthy and virile, active and useful, balanced and happy in their work', most would have understood the motivation that lay behind such enthusiasm. More in keeping with *Werkbund* thinking was Corbusier's cult of the everyday object, and when he wrote 'Our modern life . . . has created its own objects: its costume, its fountain pen, its eversharp pencil, its typewriter, its telephone, its admirable office furniture, its plate-glass, and its "innovation" trunks, the safety razor and the briar pipe, the bowler hat and limousine, the steamship and the airplane', his pronouncements have a distinctly *Werkbund* ring.

This acceptance of the twentieth-century environment, the conviction that beauty, significance, order and objectivity were manifested in its everyday objects, as well as in its engineering achievements, and the preoccupation with equivalences between the Greek and contemporary experience are fundamental to Continental design and architectural theory in the first decades of the twentieth century. While Lethaby was exploring his ideal of the commonplace, the concept of 'modernity' and its apt expression in a machine aesthetic were analysed in journals such as *L'Esprit Nouveau* and, in a less iconoclastic vein, in the yearbooks of the *Deutscher Werkbund* which were published annually from 1912 to 1915. The yearbooks carried articles by prominent *Werkbund* members such as Muthesius, Gropius, Behrens and Riemerschmid; they included photographs of applied and graphic design which confirm that there was, at that stage, no coherent *Werkbund* style; the monumental and the trivial predominate, and within this context the achievements of Van de Velde and Riemerschmid seem outstanding—far more sophisticated than contemporary work by Gropius and Behrens. But although the yearbooks have obvious similarities with the *Studio*, they completely break from the art journal precedent in the inclusion, among the photographs, of illustrations of cars and locomotives, liners, bridges, railway stations and aeroplanes, and in the tone and content of some of the articles which accepted the technological revolution, and assumed that the engineer could make as valid a contribution to a contemporary design aesthetic as the artist/craftsman. There are certain analogies here with contemporary Futurist polemics; the more radical members of the *Werkbund*, however, were in no way anarchistic, and they anticipated the purists of the '20s in their admiration for the Greeks. Greece was to them synonymous with order, clarity, logic and discipline, and Greek architecture was a demonstration of these virtues. Such architecture was controlled and rational, pure and predictable; its creators were concerned, not with self-expression but with the eternal concepts of space, structure and harmony, concepts which could be expressed by the use of predetermined orders. Ornament which arose from the use of these orders was in itself logical, and as such, justifiable. The recognition of a need to establish a rational order and clearly defined standards in architecture and design was therefore inherent in *Werkbund* thinking prior to World War I; engineering design was admired and approved because it was a scientific discipline, subject to mathematically defined laws. The men who built the bridges, locomotives, aeroplanes and liners that were documented in the yearbooks could not afford to be subjective, for in these areas 'style' was both determined by and expressive of function and materials; the forms thus achieved, however, were inherently beautiful, just as Greek architecture was beautiful. Architects, too, should welcome contemporary scientific disciplines if they were to produce work that was socially viable and to achieve a harmony and beauty that was expressive of the new society, for architecture was both a science and the highest form of art. These theories, which were suggested in various *Werkbund* articles, notably those of Gropius, were fully elaborated in Corbusier's *Vers une Architecture*, which extends and distils this aspect of *Werkbund* thinking. 'Architecture', wrote Corbusier, 'is governed by standards. Standards are a matter of logic, analysis and precise study. Standards are based on a problem which has been well-stated . . . We must first of all aim at the setting up of standards in order to face the problem of perfection.'

This preoccupation with perfection and the conviction that it could be achieved by harnessing and harmonizing the potentials of modern life is characteristic of design theory in the '20s. It is inherent in both de Stijl and Bauhaus ideology, but the latter inherited conflicts that the *Werkbund*, in spite of the convictions of its more radical members, had not entirely resolved. For the *Werkbund*, as an association of artists, craftsmen, theorists and industrialists dedicated to the improvement of both craft and industrial design, contained within its theory opposing definitions of perfection, and conflicting attitudes as to how and why it should be achieved. 'The setting up of standards' was its fundamental aim, but the attempt to define these standards split the *Werkbund* into two opposing factions. On the one hand there were the individualists who upheld the claims of the *Jugendstil* by insisting that the artist was a free agent in whatever medium he worked, and on the other were those who insisted on standardization in the interests both of art and economy. Champion of the subjective approach was Henry Van de Velde, who, at the invitation of the Grand Duke, had been working in Weimar since 1902, and who had established the arts and crafts school there that was to become the Bauhaus. His 'opponent' was Muthesius, dedicated to the promotion of German trade and patron of young and *avant garde* architects such as Walter Gropius, Peter Behrens, Hans Poelzig and Bruno Paul.[45] The Cologne exhibition provided both protagonists with a platform to air their views, and at the *Werkbund*'s annual meeting in 1914 they defined their attitudes in open debate.[46] Muthesius opened the meeting with his classic defence of standardization. 'Architecture', he said, 'together with all the activities of the *Werkbund*, is moving towards standardization (*Typisierung*); only by means of standardization can it achieve that universality characteristic of ages of harmonious culture.' Only through standardization, he continued, could a style be achieved that was both universal and significant, a style that would establish Germany as a leading nation both in trade and culture. To this end he called for propaganda to publicize German achievements abroad and for support for exhibitions to promote the best German work; the primary aim of the *Werkbund*, he insisted, was to purify and ennoble German production and thus to establish an export trade in German design.

To Van de Velde, on the other hand, such preoccupations smacked of materialism and betrayal: 'So long as there are artists within the *Werkbund*,' he declared, 'and so long as they are able to influence its fate, they will protest against the imposition of orders or standardization. The artist is, in essence, a total individualist, a free, spontaneous creator: he will never, of his own accord, submit to a discipline which imposes on him a canon or a type.' Standardization to Van de Velde, therefore, was synonymous with sterility; it implied a castration of creative talent, and in Germany, he maintained, there was no dearth of creativity—creativity, moreover, that was both spontaneous and truly expressive of its epoch. For Van de Velde rejected the philosophic content of Muthesius' arguments just as vehemently as he denounced its materialism; nothing good, he insisted, could be created for materialistic ends, and the demands of the export market were immaterial. Tiffany glass, Copenhagen porcelain, Jensen silverware and the books of Cobden-Sanderson were not designed for export, but because there would always be a demand for the best, they were being exported to Germany. And he was in agreement with Muthesius on one point: that it was the function of the *Werkbund* to promote the best. 'Each exhibition', he concluded, 'must have one aim—that of demonstrating native quality to the world, and *Werkbund* exhibitions are only relevant when, as Herr Muthesius so aptly states, they concentrate on excellence, and on the best.'

The success of the Cologne exhibition, however, proved a vindication of *Werkbund* aims, for although the *Typenmöbel* were its only significant contribution, at that time, to product design, its architectural innovations were perhaps the most significant of the century. It included important experimental work by Gropius, Behrens and Bruno Taut, as well as buildings by Van de Velde and Hoffmann. And even before World War I the *Werkbund* was sufficiently well known to inspire similar organizations in other European countries. Austria, for example, established its *Werkbund* in 1910, and the Swiss *Werkbund* was founded in 1913; the Swedish *Slöjdsföreningen* was also reorganized along *Werkbund* lines during this period, and the DIA, as we have seen was founded in 1915. 'Where an enemy has a noble lesson to teach', stated Clutton Brock, 'it can only be learned from him nobly.'[47]

Each of these groups had its own contribution to make to native design and design theory. None, however, could match the achievements of the German *Werkbund* which was able to sponsor the Weissenhof development—a demonstration of international ideals in domestic architecture—in 1927; while three years later the *Werkbund* display section in the Paris exhibition vindicated the ideals of the Bauhaus at a time when the National Socialists were threatening its closure.

8   Consolidation or eclipse?

When Lethaby died in 1931 the inscription 'Love and labour are all' was carved on his gravestone. Such a doctrine, implying both altruism and the ideal of personal fulfilment, had inspired the British design reform movement for nearly a century. By 1930, however, it seemed that British designers and architects had loved and laboured in vain, and that the Arts and Crafts movement, instead of promoting its ultimate goal of reconciling art and technique, had spawned a progeny of cranks and eccentrics, the 'arty crafty' with their aura of the homespun and the country dance.

In spite of the efforts of the Gorell Committee, the Pick Council, the DIA and Sir Herbert Read,[1] Britain had failed to produce either a *Werkbund* or a Bauhaus; its reformers made little impression on industry, for few British industrialists possessed the *Werkbund* spirit—new ideas in design, it seemed, were not worth sponsoring, in the interests either of art or economics. And rather than be involved in what Lethaby called 'matters of national strength, efficiency and pride',[2] such latter-day manifestations as Eric Gill's communities and the Omega workshops, however laudable their aims, only served to emphasize the isolation of the artist/craftsman and to set him apart from the rest of the community, so that it was in the field of printing and typography alone that Britain had any positive contribution to make to international developments. 'For the first twelve years after the war', wrote Nikolaus Pevsner in 1937,[3] 'one can hardly speak of a live Modern Movement in English architecture and industrial art.' Pevsner's *Enquiry into Industrial Art in England* painted a depressing picture of British design in the '30s. ('Things are extremely bad,' he wrote. 'When I say that 90 per cent of British industrial art is devoid of any aesthetic merit, I am not exaggerating.') And although he softened the blow by pointing out that deplorable standards were not confined to Britain, it was obvious that Germany had been far more successful in promoting the concept of industrial design, and that the Scandinavians were in fact demonstrating the Arts and Crafts ideals in action.

By 1920 Scandinavian designers had already laid firm foundations for their postwar achievements. In Denmark Georg Jensen had by 1905, begun to produce the silverware that Van de Velde so admired; as early as 1917 Kaare Klint was engaged in anthropometric research, planning a system of desks, bookcases, filing cabinets and shelf units, whose dimensions were based on sheet paper sizes; he was later to continue this type of work with domestic storage furniture, and in 1924 was appointed lecturer in the newly formed department of furniture at the Copenhagen Academy of Art. The Academy was associated with the work of designers such as Mogens Koch, Ole Wanscher, Arne Jacobsen, Børge Mogensen and Poul Kjaerholm, and with the support of the Cabinetmakers' Guild of Copenhagen they were to promote and realize the ideals for furniture design that the Arts and Crafts movement had formulated. Their aim was to equate functional efficiency with perfection of form and finish, and since they shared the social preoccupations of their British predecessors, to produce decent and inexpensive domestic furniture. Although furniture of this kind can never be cheap, these craftsmen/designers gradually began to influence factory production and to introduce machine techniques into their workshops. During this same period a similar 'renaissance' was taking place throughout the Danish craft-based industries; the *Kritisk Revy* (*Critical Review*), for example, was founded in 1926, and although it was primarily an architectural magazine, its editor Poul Henningsen used it to launch an attack on the consumer goods industries, and to accuse his 'craftsmen friends' of ignoring their 'obligations to the modern world'. 'We have no proper tumblers, plates, water-sets, spoons, knives or forks', he wrote, 'while richer homes are flooded with trash and rubbish at fantastic prices!'[4] His advice—'Simply make things which are fit for use'—was taken up by such designers as Kay Bojensen, Nathalie Krebs and Marie Gudme Leth, who were working in silver and metalware, ceramics and textiles, Bojensen echoing the ideals of the English Arts and Crafts movement by insisting that 'The things we make should have life and heart in them, and be a joy to hold. They must be human, vital and warm.'[5]

John Sedding's vision of 1888 that the designer 'should be part of the working staff of the factory, see his designs take shape, and be consulted as required' was being realized, in the inter-war years, in the other Scandinavian countries. Sweden's contribution is closely linked with the work of the *Svenska Slöjdsföreningen*, the Swedish Society of Industrial Design, which was founded in the mid-nineteenth century in order to establish a school of art and craftsmanship. By the 1890s, when Sweden was beginning to exploit her natural resources, to extend her factories and her saw-mills and to expand her glass and ceramics industries, a national style was slowly beginning to emerge, and the social priorities that the *Slöjdsföreningen* was to champion were being established. In 1897, for example, an Industrial Exhibition was held in Stockholm, and the painter, Carl Larsson, exhibited watercolours of domestic interiors which were published in his book *Ett Hem* (*A Home*) two years later; also in 1897 Ellen Key had written a series of pamphlets on the theme *Beauty for All*, demanding 'domestic equipment that fulfils the most vital requirements—namely, that everything should answer the purpose it was intended for. A chair should be comfortable to sit on, a table comfortable to work or eat at, a bed good to sleep in.'[6] The *Svenska Slöjdsföreningen* was not to embark on its systematic programme of anthropometric research until the 1950s and '60s, when Gotthard Johansson and Erik Berglund began their investigations into the functional requirements of the home and its equipment,[7] but the society had set the pattern for its future development long before this. It had organized its first exhibition of 'industrial art' in 1909, then, prompted by the success of the *Deutscher Werkbund*, had intensified its campaign to promote better standards in industrial design. In 1917 it organized a competition for furnishing a series of small apartments at low cost, and exhibited the results in Stockholm, declaring in Muthesian terms that the aim of the exhibition was 'to stimulate the production of types and models suited to mass-production and therefore inexpensive, yet in good taste', and that the 'collaboration of industry with art is now more important than ever'.[8] After this the *Slöjdsföreningen* began to act as a liaison between the craftsman and industry, so that the Swedish consumer goods industries established a tradition of working with designers, an experience that was to be reflected in its export figures after World War II. Simon Gate had joined the Orrefors glass-works as early as 1916, and Edward Hald was working both for Orrefors and for Rörstrand in 1917, the same year that Wilhelm Kåge joined the Gustavsberg works.

Developments in Norway and Finland followed a similar pattern; the Norwegian *Brukskunst* (Applied Art Association) was founded in 1918, and like its Swedish and German equivalents, was soon playing a positive rôle in establishing a national style in that country's craft-based industries. The Finnish craft revival stems from the 1870s; the Central School of Arts and Crafts was founded in Helsinki in 1871; in 1875 it sponsored the Society of Crafts and Design which took over the management of the school in order to promote its ideals over a wider field, while a third force came into play with the formation of the Friends of Finnish Handicraft in 1879. By the 1890s an awareness of Finnish work was spreading throughout Europe; Axel Gallén, who had trained as a painter at the Académie Julian was designing textiles, ceramics, furniture and jewellery, and in 1900 he and Eliel Saarinen designed the Finnish Pavilion at the Paris Exposition. Gallén (who later changed his name to the more Finnish-sounding Akseli Gallén-Kallela) introduced a fellow-student from Julians, the Swedish Louis Sparre, to Finland, and together they founded the 'Iris' shop and workshops to sell their own designs and other examples of 'modern industrial art'. Sparre kept in touch with contemporary European developments by reading the *Studio* (he contributed an article on Finnish Art in 1896) and by travelling abroad. He had seen the Red House, for example, and it was while he was visiting the World Exhibition in Brussels in 1897 that he met A. W. Finch, the Anglo-Belgian painter and potter, and persuaded him to work for 'Iris'. Willy Finch, much admired by Van de Velde,[9] remained in Finland and taught at the Central School until the '20s. These were the forerunners; the next generation, men like Alvar Aalto, Kaj Franck, Timo Sarpaneva and Tapio Wirkkala consolidated the pioneering aims of Iris by their experimental work both in craft design and mass production.

By the 1950s, therefore, the Scandinavians had accomplished all that the Arts and Crafts movement had planned to accomplish some seventy years earlier. They had used their rich natural resources to realize Morris's ideal of a 'decorative, noble, *popular* art' and because their concern went beyond appearance and finish, their pioneering work in anthropometric research provided a vital service for architects, designers and industry. Their industries, small concerns by international standards, respect their designers and artists and allow them freedom to experiment. The designers work as craftsmen and advisers, and if necessary they supervise the production processes, so that they are part of the factory and yet retain their independence. Of all the countries in Europe, the Scandinavians were, of course, in a unique position to exploit this essentially humanistic tradition. Their industries were craft-based, the Industrial Revolution did not scar them, so that they were able, when necessary, to absorb the advantages of technical change, and their work needed no proselytizing to establish its validity.

The birth pangs of the design profession in England, on the other hand, were long and laboured, and in spite of their native traditions the industrial designers of the '20s and '30s had virtually to teach themselves the first principles of their trade. Such sympathetic patrons as Heals, the Orient Line, James Powell & Sons, Barlow and Jones, and Wedgwoods, were exceptional, and Gordon Russell, who probably did more than any other individual to promote the British profession in its initial stages has described the kind of vacuum he was working in in the '20s in his auto-biography *Designer's Trade*. 'It must be remembered', he wrote, 'that in the 1920s no school of art, so far as I am aware, had accepted the principle that designing for the machine needed a very different training from designing for hand production. Most of the schools were in charge of painters, who cradled in Arts and Crafts Society theories, were antagonistic to industry and did not hesitate to say so. Industry naturally reacted by ignoring their existence.'[10] When British designers did begin to make the breakthrough, their values were conditioned, on the one hand by Arts and Crafts humanism, and on the other by the Purist rejection, or reinterpretation of this humanism. For the Continental theorists' cult of the machine-made as a celebration of the unique achievement of modern man could not be ignored, and British designers, therefore, felt themselves faced with two seemingly irreconcilable sets of values. 'The danger we run in a machine age', wrote Sir Herbert Read in 1946, 'is that we sacrifice one set of values—the personal, symbolic and decorative values—and confine art to an intellectual preoccupation with form and function.'[11]

Today, it is difficult for us to appreciate the urgency of this dilemma; the issues no longer seem so emotive, the need to make value judgements less imperative, and the problem of whether a machine can be or produce a work of art irrelevant. The missionary age has passed; neither the craftsman nor the industrial designer feels the need to defend his rôle, or to insist that his way is the right one. For the generation that inherited the conviction that ethics and aesthetics were in some way inseparable, and the belief that it is the designer's responsibility to give the public what it ought to want, has begun to question these assumptions, attempting with the help of social and psychological sciences to see people as they really are, not as they would like them to be. This determination to put the credos of the modern movement to the test has led to a more profitable collaboration with the scientific disciplines, to a relaxation in the crusade for 'good' design, and to an acceptance of individuality as well as fun and frivolity in design. While the crisis of man *versus* technology remains, however, a common vein of idealism will link the nineteenth- and twentieth-century philosophies.

Select bibliography

Relevant articles and books are also referred to in *Sources and notes*; the information is repeated here where key texts are involved.

Contemporary books and commentaries (*c. 1835–1935*)

Arts and Crafts Essays by members of the Arts and Crafts Exhibition Society Longmans Green & Co, 1893

Ashbee, Charles Robert
    Chapters in Workshop Reconstruction and Citizenship Essex House Press, 1894
    An Endeavour towards the Teaching of J. Ruskin and W. Morris Essex House Press, 1901
    Socialism and Politics Essex House Press, 1906
    Craftsmanship in Competitive Industry Essex House Press, 1908
    Modern English Silverwork Essex House Press, 1909
    The Guild of Handicraft Essex House Press, 1909
    Should We Stop Teaching Art? Batsford, 1911

Cobden-Sanderson, T. J.
    The Arts and Crafts Movement Hammersmith Publishing Society, 1905

Cole, Sir Henry
    Fifty Years of Public Work 2 vols, G. Bell & Sons, 1884

Crane, Walter
    The Claims of Decorative Art Lawrence & Bullen, 1892
    The Bases of Design G. Bell & Sons, 1898
    Line and Form G. Bell & Sons, 1900
    Ideals in Art G. Bell & Sons, 1905
    An Artist's Reminiscences Methuen, 1907
    William Morris to Whistler G. Bell & Sons, 1911

Day, Lewis F.
    Everyday Art: Short Essays on the ArtsNot-Fine London, 1882
    The Anatomy of Pattern B. T. Batsford, 1887
    The Planning of Ornament B. T. Batsford, 1887
    The Application of Ornament B. T. Batsford, 1888
    'William Morris and his Art' Easter Art Annual of the *Art Journal* 1899

Dresser, Christopher
    Rudiments of Botany London, 1859
    Unity in Variety London, 1859
    The Art of Decorative Design Day & Sons, 1862
    Principles in Design articles in *The Technical Educator*, 2 vols, 1870
    Principles of Decorative Design Cassell, Petter & Galpin, 1873
    Studies in Design London, 1876
    Principles of Art London, 1881
    Japan: its Architecture, Art and Art Manufactures London, 1882
    Ernest Gimson, His Life and Work Stratford-on-Avon, 1924

Hueffer, Ford Madox
    Ford Madox Brown, A Record of his Life and Work Longmans Green & Co, 1896

Hunt, William Holman
    Pre-Raphaelitism and the Pre-Raphaelite Brotherhood 2 vols, Macmillan, 1905–6
Johnston, Edward
    Writing and Illuminating and Lettering Pitman, 1906
Jones, Owen
    The Grammar of Ornament Day & Son, 1856
Le Corbusier
    Vers une Architecture Paris, 1923; translation *Towards a New Architecture* London, 1923
Lethaby, W. R.
    Architecture, Mysticism and Myth Percival & Co, 1892; rewritten for serialization in *The Builder* 1928; republished as *Architecture, Nature and Magic* Duckworth, 1956
    Morris as Work-Master John Hogg, 1902
    Architecture Home University Library, Williams and Norgate, 1911
    Form in Civilisation OUP, 1922
    Philip Webb and his Work OUP, 1935
    Scrip's and Scraps n.d.
Mackail, J. W.
    The Life of William Morris 2 vols, Longmans Green & Co, 1899; reissued Worlds Classics, OUP, 1950
Mackmurdo, A. H.
    'History of The Arts and Crafts Movement' preliminary typescript with additional MS preface and notes, William Morris Gallery, Walthamstow.
    'Autobiographical Notes' William Morris Gallery, Walthamstow
    A People's Charter or The Terms of Prosperity and Freedom within a Community Williams and Norgate, 1933
Massé, H. J. L. J.
    The Art Workers' Guild 1884–1934 Shakespeare Head Press, 1935
Morris, May (ed)
    The Collected Works of William Morris Longmans Green & Co, 24 vols, 1910–15
National Association for the Advancement of Art and its Application to Industry; Transactions, Liverpool, 1888; Edinburgh, 1889.
Pugin, A. N. W.
    Contrasts London, 1836; reissued Leicester Univ Press, 1969
    The True Principles of Pointed or Christian Architecture, London, 1841; reprinted St Barnabas Press, Oxford, 1969
    An Apology for the Revival of Christian Architecture in England, London, 1843; reprinted St Barnabas Press, Oxford, 1969
Redgrave, Richard
    Manual of Design Chapman & Hall, 1876
Rothenstein, Sir William
    Men and Memories 2 vols, Faber & Faber, 1931
Ruskin, John
    The Complete Works of John Ruskin 39 vols, eds E. T. Cook and A. Wedderburn, London, 1903–12
Sedding, John D.
    Art and Handicraft Kegan Paul, Trench, Trübner & Co, 1893
Semper, Gottfreid
    Wissenscrhaft, Industrie und Kunst Braunschweig, 1852; reissued Kupferberg, Mainz, 1966.
Stirling, A. M. W.
    William De Morgan and his Wife Butterworth, 1922
Wornum, Ralph
    Analysis of Ornament Chapman & Hall, 1856

Contemporary Reports, Journals and Catalogues

The Art Journal 1839–1912
The Artworkers' Quarterly 1902–6
The Cabinet-maker 1880–1936
The Furniture Gazette 1873–93

Jahrbücher des Deutschen Werkbundes 1912–15
The Journal of Design and Manufacture 1849–52
The Studio 1893 onwards

Report from the Select Committee on Arts and their connection with Manufactures, with
  the minutes of evidence; House of Commons, 9 September 1835
Catalogue of the Collection of Martinware formed by Mr Frederick John Nettlefold C. R.
  Beard, 1936

Literature since 1935

Aslin, Elizabeth
  Nineteenth-century English Furniture Faber & Faber, 1962
  The Aesthetic Movement Elek, 1969
Banham, Reyner
  Theory and Design in the First Machine Age Architectural Press, 1960
Bell, Quentin
  The Schools of Design Routledge & Kegan Paul, 1963
Bøe, Alf
  From Gothic Revival to Functional Form Oslo University Press, 1957; Basil Blackwell,
  1957
Briggs, Asa (ed)
  William Morris: Selected Writings and Designs Penguin Books, 1962
Clark, Sir Kenneth
  The Gothic Revival John Murray, 1962; Penguin Books, 1964
  Ruskin Today John Murray, 1964; Penguin Books, 1967
Cole, G. D. H. (ed)
  William Morris: Selected Writings Nonesuch Press, 1948
Deutscher Werkbund
  Fünfzig Jahre Deutscher Werkbund Alfred Metzner Verlag, Frankfurt-am-Main, 1958
Ferriday, Peter (ed)
  Victorian Architecture Cape, 1963
Franklin, Colin
  The Private Presses Studio Vista, 1969
Gaunt, William, and M. D. E. Clayton-Stamm
  William De Morgan Studio Vista, London, 1971; New York Graphic Society Ltd,
  Greenwich, 1971
Giedion, Sigfried
  Mechanization Takes Command OUP 1948
Henderson, Philip (ed)
  Letters of William Morris to his family and friends Longmans Green & Co, 1950
  William Morris: his life, work and friends Thames and Hudson, 1967
Klingender, F. D.
  Art and the Industrial Revolution edited and revised by Arthur Elton, Evelyn, Adams
  and Mackay, 1968
Macdonald, Stuart
  The History and Philosophy of Art Education University of London Press, 1970
Madsen, S. Tschudi
  Sources of Art Nouveau Oslo, New York, 1956
  Art Nouveau World University Library, Weidenfeld and Nicolson, 1967
Mumford, Lewis
  Technics and Civilization Routledge & Kegan Paul, 1934
Pevsner, Sir Nikolaus
  Pioneers of Modern Design London, 1936; Penguin Books, 1960
  Industrial Art in England CUP, 1937
  The Sources of Modern Architecture and Design Thames and Hudson, 1968
  Studies in Art, Architecture and Design Vol. 2, Thames and Hudson, 1968
  Ruskin and Viollet-le-Duc Walter Neurath Memorial Lecture, Thames and Hudson, 1969
Read, Sir Herbert
  Art and Industry Faber & Faber, 1934
Rosenberg, John
  The Darkening Glass: A Portrait of Ruskin's Genius Routledge & Kegan Paul, 1963

Russell, Sir Gordon
  Designer's Trade Allen & Unwin, 1968
Schaefer, Herwin
  The Roots of Modern Design Studio Vista, London, 1970; Praeger Publishers Inc.,
  New York, 1971
Schmutzler, Robert
  Art Nouveau Thames and Hudson, 1964
Segerstad, Ulf Hård af
  Modern Finnish Design Weidenfeld and Nicolson, 1969
Wakefield, Hugh
  Victorian Pottery Herbert Jenkins, 1962
Watkinson, Raymond
  William Morris as Designer Studio Vista, London, 1967; Van Nostrand Reinhold,
  New York, 1967
  Pre-Raphaelite Art and Design Studio Vista, London, 1970; New York Graphic
  Society Ltd, Greenwich, 1971
Williams, Raymond
  Culture and Society 1780–1950, Penguin Books, 1961
Wardle, Patricia
  Victorian Silver and Silver Plate Herbert Jenkins, 1963
Zahle, Erik (ed)
  Scandinavian Domestic Design Methuen, 1963

Catalogues

Catalogue of an Exhibition of Victorian and Decorative Arts Victoria and Albert Museum,
  HMSO, 1952
A. H. Mackmurdo and the Century Guild Collection William Morris Gallery, Walthamstow,
  1967
Catalogue of the Morris Collection William Morris Gallery, Walthamstow, 1969
Ernest Gimson Leicester Museums and Art Gallery, 1969

Sources and notes

Introduction

1 Article in *Commonweal* April 1885. Quoted from *William Morris, Selected Writings and Designs* ed Asa Briggs, Penguin Books, 1962, p 141
2 Lewis Mumford *Technics and Civilisation* Routledge & Kegan Paul, 1934
3 C. R. Ashbee 'Memoirs', unpublished typescript, 1938, Vol IV, Victoria and Albert Museum Library, p 201
4 Thorstein Veblen *The Theory of the Leisure Class* The Macmillan Company, 1899; Mentor Edition, The New American Library, 1953, p 115
5 F. T. Marinetti, lecture to the Lyceum Club, March 1912. Quoted from Reyner Banham *Theory and Design in the First Machine Age* The Architectural Press, 1960, p 123
6 László Moholy-Nagy *The New Vision* George Wittenborn, Inc, 1947, p 16
7 Quoted from Hans L. C. Jaffé *De Stijl* Thames and Hudson, 1970, p 97
8 Reyner Banham *op cit*, p 12
9 László Moholy-Nagy *op cit*, p 17

1 The sources

1 Walter Crane *William Morris to Whistler* G. Bell & Sons, 1911. Quoted from 'The English Revival in Decorative Art', first published in *Fortnightly Review*, p 54
2 John Dyer *The Fleece* 1757. Quoted from F. D. Klingender *Art and the Industrial Revolution* Evelyn, Adams & Mackay; revised and extended edition, 1968, p 13
3 See Alf Bøe *From Gothic Revival to Functional Form* Oslo University Press, 1967; Basil Blackwell, Oxford, p 32
4 A. W. N. Pugin *An Apology for the Present Revival of Christian Architecture in England* 1843
5 A. W. N. Pugin *True Principles of Pointed or Christian Architecture* 1841
6 A. W. N. Pugin *op cit*
7 *Journal of Design and Manufacture* 1849–52
8 Quoted from *Victorian Architecture* ed Peter Ferriday, Jonathan Cape, 1963. See 'C. F. A. Voysey', John Brandon-Jones, p 271
9 J. D. Sedding *Art and Handicraft* Kegan Paul, Trench, Trübner & Co, 1893. Reprint of 'Our Arts and Industries' a paper read at the Liverpool Art Congress, 1888, p 144
10 A. W. N. Pugin *An Apology for the Present Revival of Christian Architecture in England* 1843
11 Herbert Read *Art and Industry* Faber & Faber, 1934
12 *Ibid* p 21
13 A report from the Select Committee on Arts and their connection with Manufactures, with the minutes of evidence. House of Commons, 9 September 1835
14 For further analyses of the 'politics' of the Select Committee, see Quentin Bell *The Schools of Design* Routledge & Kegan Paul, 1963, and Stuart Macdonald *The History and Philosophy of Art Education* University of London Press, 1970

15 *Fifty Years of Public Work* Sir Henry Cole, London, 1884. Unfinished at Cole's death; completed and published by his son
16 *The Collected Works of John Ruskin* eds Cook and Wedderburn, London, 1903–12. *Fors Clavigera*, Letter 79
17 From *Lectures on the Results of the Great Exhibition* London, 1853
18 'Universal Infidelity in Principles of Design' *The Times*, reprinted in the *Journal of Design* Vol V, 1851
19 See Robert Schmutzler *Art Nouveau* Thames and Hudson, 1964, p 228
20 See Elizabeth Aslin *The Aesthetic Movement* Elek, 1969, p 61
21 *Manual of Design* Richard Redgrave, compiled by his son from Redgrave's writings and addresses, Chapman & Hall, 1876, p 15 *et passim*
22 *The Collected Works of John Ruskin op cit.* Preface to *Laws of Fesole*, Vol XV

2 Ruskin's 'new road'

Since the Cook and Wedderburn edition of *The Collected Works of John Ruskin* is probably not accessible to the general reader, and since so many different editions of Ruskin have been produced, most of the references here give the name of the book, the relevant chapter or lecture heading and Ruskin's own paragraph numbering. Similarly while most of William Morris's theoretical writing appears in Vol XXII of the *Collected Works*, edited by May Morris, reference is made, where appropriate, to selections which may be more easily available.

1 Speech at the Manchester Athenaeum, November, 1847; from *English Traits, The Complete Prose Works of Ralph Waldo Emerson* Ward, Lock & Co, 1890, p 309
2 'Ability' *English Traits* Ward, Lock & Co, 1890, p 251
3 'First Visit to England' *English Traits* Ward, Lock & Co, 1890, p 232
4 *Ibid*, p 236
5 Quoted from F. O. Matthiessen *American Renaissance* OUP, 1941, p 154
6 *Ibid*, p 154
7 *Ibid*, p 152
8 From William Morris *Chants for Socialists* 1885; quoted from *Wiliam Morris, Selected Writings and Designs* ed Briggs, p 115
9 From *The Two Paths* Lecture IV, nos 101 and 134
10 From *Modern Painters* Vol V, part ix, chap i, no 7
11 Walter Gropius *The Scope of Total Architecture* Harper and Row, New York, 1953; Allen & Unwin, London, 1956
12 A. H. Mackmurdo 'History of the Arts and Crafts Movement' unpublished typescript in possession of The William Morris Gallery, Walthamstow, London, E17
13 Ford M. Hueffer *Ford Madox Brown, a Record of his Life and Works* Longmans, Green & Co, 1896, p 151
14 *The Collected Works of John Ruskin* eds Cook and Wedderburn, Vol XVI, Appendix II, p 432
15 *Ibid.* From Ruskin's Evidence to Public Institutions Committee, 1860; Vol XVI, pp 472–87
16 Published as *The Political Economy of Art* 1857; reprinted with the ironic title *A Joy for Ever (and its Price in the Market)* 1880
17 From *The Two Paths* Lecture III, no 81
18 From *The Crown of Wild Olive* Lecture II, no 76
19 Leading article in the *Manchester Examiner and Times* 2 October 1860; quoted from Kenneth Clark *Ruskin Today* Penguin Books, 1967, p 265
20 *The Collected Works of John Ruskin* eds Cook and Wedderburn, Vol XVIII, p xxviii
21 *Ibid* p xxxii
22 *On the Road* Vol I, No 291
23 *The Collected Works of John Ruskin* eds Cook and Wedderburn Vol XXV, p 48
24 *Ibid* Vol XXX
25 *Ibid*
26 *Ibid* p xxiii

27 Quoted from John D. Rosenberg *The Darkening Glass* Routledge & Kegan Paul, 1963, p 132
28 From *The Two Paths* Lecture III, no 92
29 Ford M. Hueffer *Ford Madox Brown, a Record of his Life and Works* 1896, p 150

3 Theory into practice: William Morris
1 W. R. Lethaby *Philip Webb and his Work* OUP, 1935, p 27
2 From a letter to Andreas Scheu, 5 September 1883. Quoted in *William Morris* ed Asa Briggs, 1962, p 30
3 J. W. Mackail *The Life of William Morris* 2 vols, London, 1899, Vol I, p 35
4 *Ibid* p 107
5 'Pre-Raphaelitism' reprinted in *Lectures on Architecture and Painting* (Edinburgh) November 1853; *The Collected Works of John Ruskin* Vol XII, p 157, No 132
6 W. R. Lethaby *Philip Webb and his Work* 1935, p 15
7 *Ibid* p 16
8 Georgiana Burne-Jones *Memorials of Edward Burne-Jones* London 1904
9 Quoted from Raymond Watkinson *Pre-Raphaelite Art and Design* Studio Vista, 1970, p 170
10 William Holman Hunt *Pre-Raphaelitism and the Pre-Raphaelite Brotherhood* 2 vols, Macmillan, 1905-6
11 Ford M. Hueffer *Ford Madox Brown, a Record of his Life and Works* 1896 *op cit*, p 161
12 *Ibid* p 425
13 *Ibid* p 196 and Raymond Watkinson *op cit* p 169. See also 'Colonel Gillum and the Pre-Raphaelites' N. Pevsner *Burlington Magazine* March 1953
14 John D. Sedding 'The Handicraft in the Old Days' *Art and Handicraft* Kegan Paul, Trench, Trübner & Co, 1893, p 80
15 Ford M. Hueffer *op cit* p 172 and p 376
16 A. H. Mackmurdo 'History of the Arts and Crafts Movement' unpublished
17 Quoted from Philip Henderson *William Morris, his Life, Work and Friends* Thames and Hudson, 1967, p 63
18 See W. R. Lethaby *Philip Webb and his Work* 1935, p 32
19 Lethaby quotes Burne-Jones as attributing this remark to Morris in *Philip Webb and his Work* 1935, p 120
20 Quoted from the prospectus of Morris, Marshall, Faulkner and Company, issued in April 1861
21 Quoted from Philip Henderson *William Morris, his Life, Work and Friends* 1967, p 70
22 Quoted from Lewis F. Day 'William Morris and his Art' Easter Art Annual of the *Art Journal* 1899, p 2
23 W. R. Lethaby *Philip Webb and his Work* 1935, pp 37-38
24 Quoted from Raymond Watkinson *William Morris as Designer* Studio Vista 1967, p 39
25 *Arts and Crafts Essays* Longmans Green & Co, 1899; reprinted 1903, p 38
26 W. R. Lethaby *Philip Webb and his Work* 1935, p 47
27 'Of Dyeing as an Art' *Arts and Crafts Essays* 1899, p 198
28 Quoted from Philip Henderson *William Morris, his Life, Work and Friends* 1967, p 235
29 Peter Floud 'English Chintz: The influence of William Morris' *CIBA Review* No 2, 1961
30 'Textiles' *Arts and Crafts Essays* 1899, p 26
31 See *Select bibliography*; Christopher Dresser published several books and manuals on design
32 W. R. Lethaby *Morris as Work-Master* James Hogg, 1902, p 9
33 'Textiles' *Arts and Crafts Essays* 1899, p 29
34 *Ibid* p 36
35 *The Collected Works of William Morris* ed May Morris, Vol XXII, 1910-15, p 261
36 Quoted from Paul Thompson *The Works of William Morris* William Heinemann, 1967, p 73
37 'The Beauty of Life' *William Morris* Centenary Edition ed G. D. H. Cole, Nonesuch Press, 1948, p 564
38 'The Lesser Arts', *ibid* p 496
39 *Ibid* p 513
40 Anecdote in W. R. Lethaby *Philip Webb and his Work* p 94. Lethaby describes Webb's

work in the 1870s at Rounton Grange for Sir Lowthian Bell: 'Sir Lowthian Bell told Mr Alfred Powell that one day he heard Morris talking and walking about in an excited way, and went to enquire if anything was wrong. "He turned on me like a mad animal"— "It is only that I spend my life in ministering to the swinish luxury of the rich."'

41 From a letter to Andreas Scheu, 1883 quoted from *William Morris: Selected Writings and Designs* ed Asa Briggs, 1962, p 32
42 From a letter to C. E. Maurice, 1883; *ibid* p 137
43 From a letter to Robert Thompson, *ibid* p 138
44 'The Beauty of Life' *William Morris* Centenary Edition ed G. D. H. Cole, Nonesuch Press, 1948, p 549
45 'Useful Work versus Useless Toil' *ibid* p 619
46 Philip Henderson *The Letters of William Morris to his Family and Friends* Longmans, Green & Co, 1950, p 375
47 'Art and Socialism' *William Morris* ed G. D. H. Cole, Nonesuch Press, 1948, p 639
48 'Art and the Beauty of the Earth' *The Collected Works of William Morris* ed May Morris Vol XXII
49 'Art and Socialism' *William Morris* ed G. D. H. Cole, Nonesuch Press, 1948, p 637
50 'How we live and how we might live' *ibid*
51 *Ibid* p 648
52 William Morris *A Factory as it might be* ed G. D. H. Cole, Nonesuch Press, 1948 (not included in *Collected Works*) p 653
53 *Ibid* p 653
54 Oscar Wilde 'The Soul of Man under Socialism' *Essays* ed Pearson, London, 1950
55 'Printing' *Arts and Crafts Essays* 1893, p 133
56 *A Note by William Morris on his aims in founding the Kelmscott Press* 1898
57 W. R. Lethaby *Morris as Work-Master* 1902, p 21
58 From Colin Franklin *The Private Presses* Studio Vista, 1969, p 94
59 *Ibid* p 110
60 From P. M. Handover 'British Book Typography' *Book Typography 1815–1965* ed Kenneth Day, Ernest Benn Ltd, 1966, p 166
61 From James M. Wells 'Book Typography in the United States of America' *op cit* p 352

4 Guilds and guildsmen

1 From E. P. Thompson *William Morris, Romantic to Revolutionary* Lawrence and Wishart, 1955, p 732
2 From Robert Schmutzler *Art Nouveau* Thames and Hudson, 1964, p 153
3 *Elbert Hubbard's Scrap Book* Wm Wise and Co, New York, 1923
4 See Walter Crane 'Arts and Crafts allied to Architecture' *William Morris to Whistler* G. Bell & Sons, 1911, p 132
5 From Elizabeth Aslin *The Aesthetic Movement* Elek, 1969, p 109
6 Walter Crane 'The English Revival in Decorative Art' *William Morris to Whistler* p 54
7 'The Art of the Nineteenth Century' *ibid* p 232
8 N. Pevsner *Studies in Art, Architecture and Design* Thames and Hudson, 1968, p 151
9 A. H. Mackmurdo, Autobiographical Notes, unpub, William Morris Gallery, Walthamstow
10 W. R. Lethaby *Philip Webb and his Work* 1935, p 72
11 William Rothenstein *Men and Memories* Vol I, Faber & Faber, 1931, p 332
12 *Ibid* p 72
13 From 'Textiles' *Arts and Crafts Essays* 1893, p 35
14 A. H. Mackmurdo 'History of the Arts and Crafts Movement' unpub, William Morris Gallery, Walthamstow
15 See S. Tschudi Madsen *Art Nouveau* Weidenfeld and Nicolson, 1967, p 102
16 From *William Richard Lethaby* ed A. R. N. Roberts, London, 1957
17 From H. J. L. J. Massé *The Art-Workers' Guild* Shakespeare Head Press, 1935, p 7
18 Walter Crane *An Artist's Reminiscences* G. Bell & Sons, 1907
19 H. J. L. J. Massé *The Art-Workers' Guild* 1935, p 47
20 *Ibid* p 81
21 *Ibid* p 4

22 *Ibid* p 10
23 J. W. Mackail *Life of William Morris* 1899 and 1950
24 *Arts and Crafts Essays op cit* p 12
25 Walter Crane, 'The English Revival in Decorative Art' *William Morris to Whistler* 1911, p 64
26 See Stuart Macdonald *The History and Philosophy of Art Education* 1970, p 296
27 *Ibid*
28 Walter Crane 'On the Study and Practice of Art' *William Morris to Whistler* 1911, p 114
29 Walter Crane *Claims of Decorative Art* G. Bell & Sons, 1892

5 Guildsmen and industry

1 See N. Pevsner 'Matthew Digby Wyatt' *Studies in Art, Architecture and Design* Vol II, pp 104–5. In the *Journal of Design*, II, 1849–50, p 72 Wyatt wrote: 'Instead of boldly recognising the tendencies of the age, which are inevitable . . . instead of considering the means of improving these tendencies . . . he either puts up his back against their further development, or would attempt to bring back the world of art to what its course of action was four centuries ago. Our course in this nineteenth century may be hateful, if you please; denounce it, but as it *is* our course, wise men should recognise the fact.'
2 The illustrated catalogue of the Paris International Exhibition, *Art Journal*, Virtue and Co, 1878
3 Walter Crane *Ideals in Art* 1905, p 30
4 *Ibid* p 31
5 Quoted from Elizabeth Aslin *The Aesthetic Movement* 1969, p 132
6 Christopher Dresser *Principles of Design* published in serial form in *The Technical Educator* Cassell, Petter and Galpin, 1872, p 277
7 *Ibid*
8 F. M. Hueffer *Ford Madox Brown, a record of his life and work* 1896, p 431
9 William De Morgan delivered a paper on lustre ware to the Society of Arts in May 1892; published in their journal 1892
10 Reginald Blunt *The Wonderful Village* London, 1918
11 C. R. Ashbee, Memoirs, 1938, Vol II, p 137
12 Quoted from Hugh Wakefield *Victorian Pottery* Herbert Jenkins, 1962, p 134
13 C. R. Ashbee, Memoirs, Vol III, p 130
14 See Hugh Wakefield *op cit*, p 134 and Reginald Blunt *op cit*
15 C. R. Ashbee, *op cit*, Vol III
16 M. D. E. Clayton-Stamm 'William De Morgan and his pottery' *Apollo* January 1967
17 J. D. Sedding *Art and Handicraft* Kegan Paul, Trench, Trübner & Co, 1893, p 76
18 *Ibid*
19 *Arts and Crafts Essays* 1893: 'Furniture' Stephen Webb, p 89; 'Furniture and the Room' Edward S. Prior, p 261; 'Of the Room and Furniture' Halsey Ricardo, p 274; 'The English Tradition' Reginald Blomfield, p 289; 'Carpenters' Furniture' W. R. Lethaby, p 302; 'Of Decorated Furniture' J. H. Pollen, p 310; 'Of Carving' Stephen Webb, p 345; 'Intarsia and Inlaid Woodwork' T. G. Jackson, p 330
20 *Ibid* p 291–2
21 Walter Crane *William Morris to Whistler* 1911, p 54
22 *Arts and Crafts Essays* 1893 pp 270 and 272
23 *The Times* 15 April 1901; quoted from S. T. Madsen *Art Nouveau* p 164
24 *Arts and Crafts Essays* 1893, pp 285–6
25 Sir Reginald Blomfield *Richard Norman Shaw RA* Batsford, 1940
26 *Ernest Gimson, His Life and Work* Basil Blackwell, 1924, p 1
27 Quoted from 'Ernest Gimson' catalogue to the Leicester Museums and Art Gallery exhibition, 1969, p 7
28 *Ernest Gimson, His Life and Work op cit* p 18
29 *Ibid* p 6
30 See 'Ernest Gimson' catalogue, *op cit* p 41
31 N. Pevsner *Pioneers of Modern Design* Penguin Books, 1960, p 152
32 'Ernest Gimson' catalogue *op cit* p 7

33 *The Builder* October 1899, p 335; quoted from Elizabeth Aslin *Nineteenth-century English Furniture* Faber & Faber, 1962, p 72
34 See B. G. Burrough 'Three Disciples of William Morris, Ernest Gimson, part II' *Connoisseur* November 1969
35 *Ernest Gimson, His Life and Work* 1924, p 14
36 *Arts and Crafts Essays* 1893, p 108
37 *Ibid* p 55
38 *Art Journal* catalogue, *op cit* 1878
39 *The Collected Works of John Ruskin op cit* Vol XXX p xxiv *et passim*
40 'Home Arts and Industries' Transactions of the National Association for the Advancement of Art and its Application to Industry, Edinburgh meeting, 1889; London, 1890, p 422
41 *Ibid* p 437
42 Other publications by W. A. S. Benson include *Drawing—its History and its Uses* (see below); *Elements of Handicraft and Design* 1893, and *Notes on Electric Wiring and Fittings* 1897
43 *Drawing—its History and its Uses*, incorporating 'A Brief Memoir of W. A. S. Benson' by W. H. Bruce, OUP, 1925
44 *The Times* 9 July 1924, quoted in *Drawing—its History and its Uses.*
45 A. H. Mackmurdo 'History of the Arts and Crafts Movement' unpublished
46 This description, of the Liverpool Congress in 1888, is from Walter Crane 'The English Revival in Decorative Art' *William Morris to Whistler* p 74
47 J. E. Hodgson 'On the Failure in Results of the Government Art Schools', Transactions of the National Association for the Advancement of Art, *op cit*, p 55
48 R. Rowand Anderson *Presidential Address*, Section of Architecture, Edinburgh Transactions, *op cit*, p 55
49 Lewis F. Day *Everyday Art: Short Essays on the Arts Not-Fine* London, 1882, pp 273–4
50 W. R. Lethaby *Philip Webb and his Work* p 79
51 John D. Sedding *Art and Handicraft* Kegan Paul, Trench, Trübner & Co, 1893
52 *Ibid* p. 129

6 Ashbee and the craft of the machine
1 C. R. Ashbee, Memoirs, Vol I, unpublished typescript, 1938. Victoria and Albert Museum Library, p 19
2 *Ibid* Vol I
3 *Ibid* Vol I, p 8
4 C. R. Ashbee *Modern English Silverwork* Essex House Press, 1909, p 6
5 Toynbee Hall, File 9, Greater London Record Office; see also 'Three Disciples of William Morris, Charles Robert Ashbee; part I' *Connoisseur* October 1969, p 88
6 C. R. Ashbee *Craftmanship in Competitive Industry* Essex House Press, 1908, p 214
7 See Shirley Bury 'An Arts and Crafts Experiment; the silverwork of C. R. Ashbee' Victoria and Albert Museum Bulletin. January 1967; Vol III, No 1, p 18
8 *Ibid*
9 C. R. Ashbee *Should we Stop Teaching Art?* London, 1911
10 C. R. Ashbee *Craftmanship in Competitive Industry* 1908, Appendix V, pp 256–8
11 *The Masque of the Edwards of England* Essex House Press, 1902. Quoted from Colin Franklin *The Private Presses* p 76
12 *Studio* Vol IX, 1896–7, p 126
13 C. R. Ashbee, Memoirs, Vol I
14 *Ibid*
15 See Horst-Herbert Kossatz 'The Vienna Secession and its early relations with Great Britain' *Studio International*, January 1971, p 12 and p 17
16 See 'Three Disciples of William Morris, C. R. Ashbee, part 2' *Connoisseur* December 1969, p 262
17 C. R. Ashbee, Memoirs *op cit*, Vol I, p 399
18 *Ibid*, Vol II, p 236
19 C. R. Ashbee *Craftsmanship in Competitive Industry* 1908, p 194
20 *Ibid*

21 Charles Rowley *A Workshop Paradise and other Papers* Sherratt & Hughes, 1905, p 4
22 C. R. Ashbee *Guild of Handicrafts* Essex House Press, 1909
23 C. R. Ashbee *Craftsmanship in Competitive Industry* 1908, p 53
24 *Ibid* p 38
25 C. R. Ashbee *Should we Stop Teaching Art?* 1911, chapter 1, p 2
26 C. R. Ashbee, Memoirs, Vol I, p 96
27 *Ibid*
28 *Ibid* p 192
29 *Ibid* p 228
30 *Ibid* p 241
31 Frank Lloyd Wright *A Testament* Horizon Press NY
32 C. R. Ashbee, Memoirs, Vol I, p 242
33 *Ibid*, p 242
34 *Ibid* pp 242, 243
35 See Alan Crawford 'Ten Letters from Frank Lloyd Wright to Charles Robert Ashbee' *Journal of Architectural Historians of Great Britain* Vol 13, 1970
36 *Ibid*
37 *Frank Lloyd Wright, The Early Work* New York, 1968, p 8. See also Alan Crawford *op cit*
38 *Ibid* and Reyner Banham *Theory and Design in the First Machine Age* Architectural Press, 1960, p 147
39 C. R. Ashbee *Should we Stop Teaching Art?* 1911, p 50

7 Towards an efficiency style

1 From Ebenezer Howard *Garden Cities of To-Morrow* Faber and Faber, 1946; preface by F. J. Osborn, p 11
2 See, for example, comments on and quotations from Adolf Loos' essays in Nikolaus Pevsner's introduction to *Adolf Loos, Pioneer of Modern Architecture* Thames and Hudson, 1966; Hermann Muthesius also enthused in *Das Englische Haus* about British plumbing, and an exhibition of 'British Craftsmanship' organized by Steen Eiler Rasmussen at the Danish Museum of Industrial Art in 1932, showed British sports equipment, leather goods, cooking utensils, etc.
3 W. R. Lethaby 'Art and Workmanship'; first published in *Imprint*, 1913. Reprinted in *Form in Civilisation* OUP, 1922, p 209
4 Quoted from Stuart Macdonald *The History and Philosophy of Art Education* 1970, p 297
5 According to B. G. Burrough in 'Three Disciples of William Morris, W. R. Lethaby' *Connoisseur* January 1971, 'Noel Rooke, an early pupil (ultimately the School's Vice-Principal) declared that he never saw Frampton at the School and only met one man who said he had'.
6 *William Richard Lethaby* ed A. R. N. Roberts, London, 1957, p 24
7 *Ibid*
8 Priscilla Johnston *Edward Johnston* Faber and Faber, 1969
9 *William Richard Lethaby* ed A. R. N. Roberts 1957
10 'Arts and Crafts' a Review of the Work executed by students in the leading art schools of Great Britain and Ireland, ed Charles Holme, *The Studio*, 1916, p 9
11 *Ibid* p 10
12 *Ibid* p 9
13 Priscilla Johnston *op cit*
14 Edward Johnston *Writing and Illuminating and Lettering* Pitman, 1906
15 W. R. Lethaby *Form in Civilisation* 1922, p 209 and p 211
16 *Idem, Scrip's and Scraps* ed Alfred H. Powell, p 28
17 *Ibid* p 50
18 *Idem, Form in Civilisation* 1922, p 111
19 *Idem, Scrip's and Scraps* n.d. p 52
20 *Ibid* p 50
21 *Idem, Morris as Workmaster* 1902
22 *Idem, Philip Webb and his Work* 1935
23 Robert W. S. Weir *William Richard Lethaby* London 1932, p 8
24 *Ibid* p 9

25 See biographical note to W. R. Lethaby *Architecture, Nature and Magic* Gerald Duck-worth & Co, 1956; Alfred Powell writes 'Those who worked with him at the British Museum and elsewhere have told of their astonishment at his instant and certain diagnosis of the probable that seldom failed to establish proof', p 12

26 'Education for Industry' *Handicraft and Reconstruction* John Hogg, 1919 p 76

27 *Ibid* p 84

28 W. R. Lethaby *Architecture* Home University Library, Williams & Norgate, 1911

29 *Ibid* p 251

30 *Ibid* p 247. See also N. Pevsner 'Lethaby's Last' *Architectural Review* November 1961, pp 354–7; Pevsner quotes a letter from Lethaby to Sydney Cockerell in which Lethaby writes that if he were able to start again he 'would eschew taste and design and all that stuff and learn engineering and hard building experience. Hardness, facts, experiments—that should be architecture, not taste.'

31 W. R. Lethaby *Form in Civilisation op cit*, p 95

32 *Ibid* p 36

33 *Ibid* p 10

34 *Ibid* p 36

35 Quoted from N. Pevsner 'The DIA' *Studies in Art, Architecture and Design* Thames and Hudson, 1968, p 228

36 *Ibid*

37 Quoted from N. Pevsner's introduction to *Adolf Loos* p 14

38 *Studio Year-Book of Decorative Art, 1914* p 94

39 *Fünfzig Jahre Deutscher Werkbund*

40 *Ibid*

41 *Ibid*

42 *Ibid*

43 *Ibid*

44 Le Corbusier *Vers une architecture* Paris and London, 1923

45 See Walter Scheidig *Crafts of the Weimar Bauhaus* Studio Vista, 1967, p 9, and N. Pevsner *Pioneers of Modern Design* p 36. On Muthesius' instigation, Behrens was appointed head of the Academy of Art in Dusseldorf; Poelzig in Breslau and Taut in Berlin

46 *Fünfzig Jahre Deutscher Werkbund*

47 N. Pevsner 'The DIA' *Studies in Art, Architecture and Design* 1968, p 228

8 Consolidation or eclipse?

1 In 1931 the Board of Trade had appointed a Committee on Art and Industry with Lord Gorell as chairman; its report was published in 1932. The Council for Art and Industry, under the chairmanship of Frank Pick, of the London Underground, was established in 1934 to suggest ways in which the recommendations of the Gorell Report could be implemented. Herbert Read's *Art and Industry* was first published by Faber in 1934.

2 W. R. Lethaby *Form in Civilisation* 1922, p 112

3 N. Pevsner *An Enquiry into Industrial Art in England* CUP, 1937, p 12

4 Quoted from *Scandinavian Domestic Design* ed Erik Zahle, Methuen & Co, 1963, p 10

5 *Ibid* p 13

6 *Ibid* p 54

7 *Bord* (*Tables for meals and work in the home*) by Erik Berglund was published by the *Svenska Slöjdsföreningen* in 1957; *Skåp* (*Cupboards—a practical study of space requirements for storage furniture*) followed in 1960. The pioneer ng work in this field, B. Akerblom *Standing and Sitting Posture*, was first published in Stockholm in 1948

8 *Scandinavian Domestic Design op cit*, p 56

9 For further details of the work of Gallen, Sparre and Finch, see *Modern Finnish Design* Weidenfeld and Nicolson, 1969

10 Gordon Russell *Designer's Trade* Allen & Unwin, 1968, p 129

11 *The Practice of Design* introduction by Herbert Read, Lund Humphries, 1946, p 13

Index